Flyball Racing

The Dog Sport for Everyone

Lonnie Olson

Howell Book House
New York
Macmillan • USA

for Karli

(U-CD, U-Agll Gelert's Karli, CKC-CDX, STD(d,s), FMCh, WETX, TT, TDI, O-VCCX, DSA)

Howell Book House
A Simon & Schuster Macmillan Company
1633 Broadway
New York, NY 10019

Library of Congress Cataloging-in-Publication Data:

Olson, Lonnie.
  Flyball racing: the dog sport for everyone/Lonnie Olson.
    p. cm.
  ISBN 0-87605-630-3
    1. Flyball (Dog sport)   I. Title
  SF425.85.F56047   1997
  798.8—dc21   97-2761
                                                CIP

Manufactured in the United States of America

        9 8 7 6 5 4 3

Book Design: designLab, Seattle
Cover Design: designLab, Seattle
Photography: Lonnie Olson, Terry Ryan, Joann Thomas, Joanne Weber.

Table of Contents

About the Author

Lonnie Olson has been active in Flyball since its early days (1983). She served on the North American Flyball Association (NAFA) Board of Directors for eight years during the formative period of the organization, helping to develop and define the rules of racing as well as the bylaws of NAFA. She is a NAFA Judge and has acted as a tournament director for her team's competitions, which have been annual events for the last twelve years. She has traveled throughout North America and Japan to give seminars and camps on Flyball training. Her efforts have greatly contributed to the spread of "Flyball fever" around the world.

Lonnie lives in Michigan with her three Border Collies and Pembroke Welsh Corgi. When she is not pursuing some dog activity, she enjoys SCUBA diving and just about any other water sport. Most of the time, however, she is involved in dog activities. Her dogs are her family, and Lonnie devotes the same time to them that most people would devote to their children.

In 1996 Lonnie founded Dog Scouts of America™. She hosts two summer camps yearly, where people can go to learn fun and functional activities with their dogs (including Flyball, of course). Lonnie has made having fun with her dogs, and helping other people have fun with their dogs, a full-time activity.

Acknowledgments

I would like to thank everyone who has contributed to the growth of the sport of Flyball in the last decade. The players, dogs and humans, the fans and the North American Flyball Association. Special thanks to my special friend, Joanne Weber, who took many of the photographs for this book. Thanks to my team, and especially to my dogs, Karli, Wile E., Koda and Weasel, for being patient with me while I wrote the book.

I would like to dedicate this book to my dog, Karli, probably the coolest dog that ever lived, and definitely the most wonderful dog I have ever had. She reads my mind, invents her own games, and she possesses logic. Karli is multi-talented and excels at every sport she tries, and she has tried almost everything. When she is not playing Flyball, she enjoys participating in Agility, herding, sled dog racing, Frisbee® catching, water rescue, backpacking and even Obedience.

For life is a game for her, and she loves to play. It was because of Karli, and dogs like her, that I founded Dog Scouts of America™. Karli is the first dog to have become a Dog Scout. For everything she has given me, I am eternally grateful.

Introduction

I started writing about Flyball in 1985. I published my first book, *Flyball: A Dog Sport For Everyone* in 1987. This was when Flyball competition was just taking off. The sport has changed a lot in the last 12 years. So much, in fact, that an entirely new book is necessary to cover all of the updated information and new training methods.

The dogs absolutely love this sport. They get so wound up getting ready to play that they can hardly control themselves. I have found that most dogs enjoy activities where they can release their energy by running full speed, chasing, catching, fetching and jumping. They must get the equivalent of what we would call a "runner's high." In addition, they get to be with all of their buddies and bark and scream wildly before the race. We handlers don't ask much of them except that they stay in their own lane before, during and after the race, and that they don't try to go until it's their turn. They show remarkable control in holding up their end of the bargain. If they didn't behave themselves, they would be left at home! If you are wondering if you and your dog would enjoy Flyball racing, I can almost guarantee that the answer is yes. The dogs think it is great fun, and the owners enjoy it because the dogs love it so much. It is also challenging for the owners to become proficient at passing and to learn strategies for maximum performance. I recommend this sport for people of all ages and dogs of every description.

One time my dog Karli and I were performing with Rock 'n' Roll K-9s. This is an entertainment production which involves demonstrations of Flyball racing, grand prix Agility racing, Frisbee® catching, pet tricks and other fun activities. I was sitting backstage between performances when Karli put her feet on the edge of my chair, and I swear she asked me, "Mom, what do the other dogs in the world do?" How could I tell her that there are other dogs that sit home all the time or live their lives on chains or in kennel runs. How could I make her understand that all dogs do not get a chance to do fun things like this with their owners. Some dogs are actually treated like less than lifelong companions and partners. Some owners actually give up their dogs because they don't want them any more. I didn't want to shatter her world, but I did want to let her know that she is a very special companion who gets to do all sorts of fun things with me because I loved her enough to make her a very educated dog. So I told her the truth: "Not all dogs get to play Flyball, honey, just the very lucky ones whose owners love them more than anything else in the world."

This book is meant to be a guide for anyone wanting to become involved in the sport of Flyball racing. I hope that the information in this book will help people in remote areas learn about the sport and train their own dogs. The sport has grown tremendously in the past decade, and I hope to see continued growth in the years to come.

Welcome to Flyball Racing

The sport of Flyball has changed dramatically over its life span of a quarter of a century. Who would have known that from its humble beginnings in someone's wood shop it would turn into the popular sport that is enjoyed by millions worldwide? With many thousands of dogs performing in sanctioned competitions and doing exhibitions for dog food company promotions, you might see Flyball at an exposition, at a dog show or on television. Flyball competition has come a long way. I have been happy to watch it grow.

What Is Flyball?

Flyball is a type of race. As a matter of fact, the word itself is often used as an adjective and it is proper to use it with another word, as in Flyball competition or Flyball training.

Flyball racing consists of teams comprised of four dogs competing against each other side by side on two separate racing lanes. The racing lanes have four jumps spaced ten feet apart, and each lane has its own Flyball box at the far end. The four dogs race one at a time, in relay fashion, until they have all finished the course with a clean run. If a dog or its handler commits a rule infraction, that dog must be rerun at the end as a fifth dog.

When Did Flyball First Appear?

The sport of Flyball reportedly originated on the West Coast in the early '70s. Someone with a ball-crazy dog invented a contraption whereby the dog could trigger a pedal on a machine and toss a ball for himself. This evolved into a relay competition (like scent hurdle racing) involving four jumps and four dogs with a Flyball box at one end. People would get together to put on Flyball demonstrations or friendly little competitions. The hard part in the early years was getting other Flyball enthusiasts and their dogs together for a race.

In the beginning, the emphasis was on catching ability. The original Flyball boxes sent the ball soaring ten or more feet into the air. This is where the term "Flyball" comes from. You wouldn't guess this by looking at Flyball racing today. In today's competitions, the emphasis is on speed. Boxes have been redesigned as a combination ball-triggering mechanism and turning surface for the dog. The canine athletes seem to turn themselves inside out, snatching the ball as they ricochet back toward the finish. A spectator is hard-pressed to even catch sight of the ball, which is snatched out of the cup so fast it is airborne for only a quarter of an inch or so.

One of the earliest commercially available Flyball boxes, the "Never Fail," built by Jim Cogswell, featured an exposed throwing arm and tuna can cup. This photo was taken in 1984 when our Flyball team was just getting started. "Quincy," owned by Clyde Moore, was one of the original team's dogs. This was before the North American Flyball Association (NAFA) came into being, so the dogs did not earn Flyball points or titles.

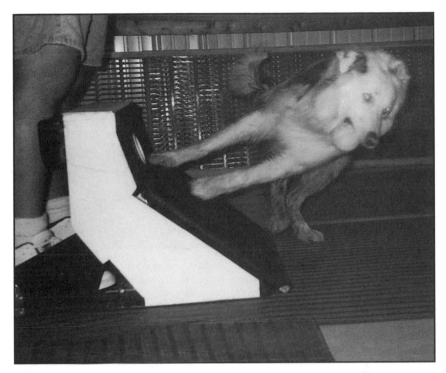

The newer style boxes feature an enclosed throwing mechanism for safety and a larger padded pedal surface, also a safety feature. The dog does not come to a stop to hit the pedal, but pivots as he catches the ball, pushing off with his front (and back) feet. He is catching and banking off the box at the same time. "Kodachrome," distinguished by the FCH, TT and DSA titles, is owned by the author.

When the rules were first written, they were only one page long. While the basics of the sport have remained the same, the rule book is now 60 pages long, covering every aspect of racing, regulations for equipment and ring dimensions, plus information regarding judging, hosting tournaments and gaining titles.

The friendly competitions have become major events performed in front of packed crowds. Sanctioned tournaments often attract hundreds of teams. Because of time and space restrictions, many hosting organizations have had to limit entries. These competitions take place on weekends, for the most part, and it is just impossible to fit in the volume of racing required when so many teams are in attendance.

Dogs become very excited about playing Flyball. Flyball involves many reinforcing behaviors for a dog: running, jumping, fetching and being excited! This White Shepherd gets so enthused watching Flyball and waiting for his turn that he bites his tongue. His owner has to hold him so he can't watch until it's his turn.

I became involved in Flyball training back in the early '80s here in Michigan. At that time, there were only a few other teams in existence. There was one in Lansing, one in Saginaw, one in Detroit and one in Ann Arbor. My team was in Flint, and these were all at least an hour's drive away, so we didn't get together often to practice. There was also a group in the Hamilton, Ontario, area that had been doing Flyball, but they were several hours away. By 1984, the teams started getting together more and having fun competitions. More teams had emerged in Michigan and Ontario, and it was not so hard to find competition. My team hosted their first tournament that year, and we managed to get seven other teams to attend.

Flyball is a growing sport. I started writing articles on Flyball training for various publications in 1984. So many people were writing to me for reprints and more information that I had to do something. For self-preservation, I published a little training manual that consisted of the collection of articles. Over 10,000 copies of this manuscript were sold all over the world, and I am proud to report that, coincidentally or consequently, the number of Flyball clubs in existence has grown incredibly over the past twelve years. At this writing, there are 400 teams regularly competing in Flyball racing.

Who Are the Participants?

The sport of Flyball is open to any breed or mixed breed. It is truly a dog sport for everyone. Dog trainers, bored with traditional competitions like Obedience, enjoy Flyball training because it is something fun and different. Handlers of all ages, from young kids to senior citizens, are involved in the sport. Your dog does not have to be a top-notch Obedience dog to excel at Flyball training. One member of my team decided to try it because his dog had flunked out of Obedience class—twice! While a modicum of obedience is necessary for control, the Flyball trainee does not need prior Obedience experience.

Why Participate?

I once had the following conversation with a "non-dog person" after I described what I do with my dogs.

> *Insurance salesman:* "I don't mean to be stupid, but *WHY* do you do this?"
>
> *Lonnie:* "Do you have kids?"
>
> Insurance salesman: "Sure."
>
> *Lonnie:* "Do you take them to their hockey or baseball games?"
>
> *Insurance salesman:* "Of course I do."
>
> *Lonnie:* "Why do you do that?"
>
> *Insurance salesman:* (silence, thinking, "Are you nuts? Dogs aren't kids!")

Some non-dog people act like dogs are supposed to be like a piece of furniture or something, instead of your companions and friends. This man couldn't understand why I would possibly want to devote so much time, effort and money playing a sport with my dogs. He probably also didn't understand why I would want to do this with not just one dog, but five of them.

Flyball competition is fun. The dogs go absolutely wild for this sport. They enjoy it so much, the owners get a big thrill out of watching them play. That's why I enjoy the sport so much. Anything my dogs want to do that much, I will do with them. We can't even say the "F" word in my house. We have to spell F-l-y-b-a-l-l or the dogs go crazy.

Border Collies will do anything to get someone to throw a ball (or anything) for them. The author's three dogs, Karli, Wile E. and Koda hold their breath in anticipation of having the ball thrown.

Flyball training is good exercise for dogs. Dogs that have been bred for a high outlay of energy in their working fields, like Border Collies and Labradors, can work off a lot of that excess energy in Flyball practice. I see many Labs and Borders in dog pounds because their unsuspecting owners were probably not prepared for the amount of mental stimulation and exercise these active breeds require. These people probably really wanted a piece of furniture, but what they got instead was a bundle of energy, and they gave this energy no outlet. This can lead to destructiveness or problem behavior that some people are ill equipped to handle.

Flyball racing is a sport with great spectator appeal. This is one sport I can watch for hours. Football confuses me and baseball bores me. Flyball competition is not only intense, fast-paced action, but the rules are not complex so it is easy to follow the game. Competitions are arranged so that teams of similar speeds race together. This means that whether you're watching a division of teams that can run under 17 seconds, or a slow division where they are lucky to finish in 30 seconds, the racing will still be fairly evenly matched. It is just as exciting to watch a "photo finish" between two evenly matched, albeit sluggish, teams as it is to watch a close heat between the really hot teams. It's all fun and nonstop action.

The author has conducted several Flyball training camps in Japan. This "Doggie Dojo" at Animal Fancier's Club features a padded rubber floor. Here they are using the K-9 Kannon Flyball boxes.

Where Are the Competitions?

Competitions are held all over the United States and Canada. The sport is gaining momentum in other countries, too, like England, Australia and Japan. If you look hard enough, I imagine you could find fellow Flyball enthusiasts in any part of the world. If not, create your own team! Just because no one has done it in your area is no reason for you not to start! This sport has a snowball effect. Once you get just a few people interested, and let it be known that you are practicing as a team, you will have other people and other teams coming out of the woodwork.

Many of the tournaments in North America take place in Michigan and Ontario, since that is where Flyball competition really got going. Some of the competitions are for fun (exhibition only) and some are sanctioned events where participants can get points toward titles or championships. For information on the competitions in your area, contact the North American Flyball Association (see Chapters 9 and 14).

How Does a Team Get Started?

To get started, get together with some friends, build or buy yourself some jumps and a Flyball box and read this book! The next chapter tells you where to find the equipment you will need, or how to build your own.

Chapter 2

Equipment Needed

The Balls

Tennis balls can be purchased at any department store, or used balls can be picked up inexpensively at a tennis club. Used balls are perfect for Flyball because they don't bounce as far. The rules state that you are not allowed to puncture the balls to take away their bounce. Most dogs can use regulation tennis balls. However, if you have Toy breeds or small dogs that prefer a smaller ball, you can use a racquet ball, squash ball, beach paddle ball or any other ball, so long as it will bounce and roll. It is against the rules to use spongy balls that just drop and lie there. Those would be too easy for the dog to pick up after a fumble. The alternate balls are not allowed to give the dogs an unfair advantage over the dogs that use tennis balls.

J & J Dog Supplies sells a small ball that is slightly less than 2 inches in diameter. This is a two-tone, cloth-covered ball, which resembles a tennis ball. You can get these by the dozen for less than $2 per ball. These are available from:

J&J Dog Supplies
P.O. Box 1517
Galesburg, IL 61402
Phone (800) 642-2050

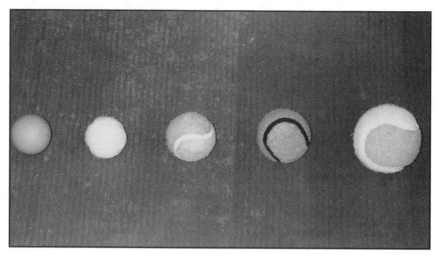

Some examples of allowable balls of varying sizes. All of these will bounce and roll. From left to right: beach paddle ball, mini tennis ball (from a key chain), Velcro mitt catch game ball, Vo-Toy ball, tennis ball. *Joanne Weber*

The Wilson tennis ball company puts out a little key chain that has a miniature tennis ball attached. By removing the key chain itself, you have a nice little tennis ball. It measures just under 1.5 inches in diameter. These balls (including key chain) are about $3 each. They are available at many athletic supply stores.

Jumps

The jumps are very easy to make, so if you are handy you don't have to order a set. In this book you will find plans for constructing your own. But there are two catalogs that sell Flyball jumps if you would rather order one:

> J & J Dog Supply
> P.O. Box 1517
> Galesburg, IL 61402
> Phone (800) 642-2050

> R.C. Steele
> 15 Turner Drive
> Spencerport, NY 14559-0140
> Phone (800) 872-3773

These companies sell two different kinds of jumps. One set is plastic and one is wooden. The building instructions in the next chapter are for the "quick and easy" jump set, which is most commonly used by Flyball teams for both practice and competition.

Boxes

Boxes can be virtually any design, provided they are mechanical (they *cannot* have an electronic release). The dimensions must be less than 24 inches wide, 18 inches high and 30 inches deep. The box must release the ball so that it will fly in the direction of the starting line, and the ball must be propelled through the air without obstruction for a distance of at least 24 inches.

Most boxes used for competition have a large, full-face pedal (or nearly full-face), an unexposed throwing arm, and one or more cups. A full-face pedal is designed such that the entire front of the box acts as a trigger—any place it is touched will set the ball. The reason for the large face is to give dogs room to turn around and shove off with their back legs at the box (like a swimmer's turn). The full-faced pedal will, of course, trigger the box no matter where the dog hits it. The enclosed throwing arm is to protect the dog from being hit in the mouth trying to get the ball out of the cup faster. The ball simply pops out of a cup in the front of the box. Some teams use boxes with several cups, so that they can accommodate various dogs and their turning preferences.

Flyball box styles have changed as much as the sport of Flyball has. The early boxes involved a pedal that was almost horizontal. The dogs would run up to the box, stop and press a pedal that was about 10 to 12 inches square. The pedals have not only gotten larger, but more vertical so that they can also be used as a turning surface. In building a box for my team, I experimented with various angles and arrived at a 70- degree angle for a banking surface. A Canadian friend who builds Flyball boxes told me that he arrived at 60 degrees as the optimum angle. You may want to experiment for yourself to arrive at the best angle for your team.

The propelling mechanism could be of any mechanical design. There are **catapult** styles, where the ball is placed into the cup on the internal throwing arm. There are **hammer** styles that strike a ball which sits in the face of the box to pop it out of the cup. There are **piston** styles that plunge the ball out of the cup using a dart gun principle. There are **plunger** styles

Various Flyball boxes currently in use. Some are homemade; some are commercially built. None feature an exposed throwing arm. All offer a large turning surface for the dogs.

that work like a crossbow or a pinball machine. There are also **paddle** styles that span the entire width of the box and strike a ball placed on a ledge at any number of points along the front. The variations and styles are limited only by the designers' imaginations.

Keep in mind that the best box for competition may not be the best box for breaking in new dogs. The "no-cup," paddle-arm, 60-degree angle pedal type of box that our team uses in competition would be a poor choice for training a new dog, as it is easy for the dog to just take the ball from the top of the box without making contact with the pedal. I prefer to break in new dogs with a 45-degree angle, full-face pedal box with an enclosed cup which is positioned 13 inches from the floor. It is a good idea to have different styles of boxes for different functions.

Depending on the amount of money you have available, you may want to start out with a homemade box. There are as many designs for Flyball boxes as there are people with ideas. If you want to build your own box, keep the regulation dimensions and function requirements in mind in case you end up using the box for competition. I have included a set of instructions for building a simple Flyball box in the next chapter. I have also provided the addresses of some manufacturers of boxes:

The Dog-a-Polt dog exercise machine. This is not advertised as a Flyball box, but can be used as one and can be obtained very inexpensively. It is lightweight and portable, too. This is definitely not a competition box. *Joanne Weber*

The Dog-a-Polt dog exercising system is an inexpensive box with a small pedal and an exposed throwing arm. It is slender, lightweight and easy to carry. The cost is around $32.95 plus shipping and handling. I wouldn't suggest it as a competition box, but for someone who is starting out and does not have a lot of money to spend, this one would be adequate to begin with. Contact:

> Dena Burnett
> 13212 NE 16th St., Suite 6
> Bellevue, WA 98005

The K-9 Kannon is another small, lightweight box. I would recommend it as a starter box or even a competition box if you can't afford one of the bigger ones. The entire face of the box is all pedal, so the dog can't miss. The box is easy to transport, but for larger dogs it might be a little small for competition. This box is well put together for the price of around $130 plus shipping and handling. Contact:

Skene Design
4843 Jeanne Mance
Montreal, PQ H2V 4J6

More examples of Flyball boxes at a tournament. Some teams personalize their boxes with their own designs and logos. The small rounded box labeled "The Pedal" (left of center) is a K-9 Kannon with some aftermarket modifications.

The Nu-style Flyball Box is an excellent competition box. It is accurate and fast. The pedal is more upright, providing a 22-inch-wide banking surface for the dogs. Most of the face of the box is the pedal. This is a heavier box, suitable for competition—however, it requires some wheels or a strong box loader! Contact:

John Grant
2079 Waycross Crescent
Mississauga, Ontario L5K 1J3
Phone (905) 822-6143

Ball Receptacles

Don't forget to choose something secure in which to hold game balls. Five-gallon buckets work well, as do tennis ball crates, but anything that holds balls will work, from a small laundry basket to a mesh bag. You will need something of adequate size to hold the balls for competition because you may need up to 35 or 40 balls per race. This would be enough for four dogs to run five heats with two warm-up runs per dog and allowing for at least one flag (rerun) per heat.

The Nu-style Flyball box, made by John Grant. Flyball is just taking off in Japan. After the first Flyball camp at Animal Fancier's Club in Japan, the group ordered 10 of these competition-quality boxes.

Mats

If you are going to have regular practices, demonstrations or competitions, you will need some rubber matting. You can get new rubber matting from J & J Dog Supply (address on page 10), or you may be able to get some used mats from a dog club or dog show superintendent in your area. When you get the mats, avoid marking them for the jump, start, and box positions. Rubber matting stretches, and the marks you put down may not stay accurate. It is better to mark the floor where you set the mat.

The backstop functions to keep loose balls from traveling out-of-bounds, or too far into the other team's box area. It is made from three sheets of 4' by 8' plywood, plus some heavy-duty hinges. Note the wood reinforcement on the hinge area. The reinforcement keeps hardware from being ripped out.

Backstop

If you are going to host competitions with your team, or even if you only plan to do demos, a backstop is a good thing to have. One can be built inexpensively from snow fence material supported by a wooden or $^3/_4$-inch polyvinyl-coated frame. This construction is also lightweight and easily portable. The purpose of the backstop is to keep the balls from bouncing too far away from the racing lanes, so the material you use must not have holes large enough to allow a ball to pass through. The backstop can actually be made of wood, or any material, but light weight and portability are important factors when constructing your Flyball equipment. You can find construction plans for a lightweight backstop in the next chapter.

Stopwatch

A Flyball team needs at least one good stopwatch. Most teams have several. The kind to buy is one with split or lap time capability. This will enable the timekeeper to track each individual dog's time at practices and tournaments for record keeping. After recording the splits, the watch will read the individual times back to you when you press the recall button.

Camcorder

This equipment is most useful in helping your team assess their dogs' passes, turns at the box, starts or anything else that requires close scrutiny. The camera can be of any make or model, but one with a running timer display is beneficial. A sturdy tripod, extra batteries and a remote are accessories that will make your filming easier.

VCR

Of course, if you have a camcorder, you will need a VCR to play back your tapes. We take ours to the tournaments with us and, after videotaping passes, we run back to the crating area to see if our pass evaluator was accurate or not. The VCR recommended is the four-head player; this kind will play back passes in slow motion or stop action, which is what you really need to accurately review and efficiently judge the speed of the dogs.

13-inch Color Television

A television is needed only if you are going to review your passes at a tournament with the VCR. Otherwise, you could wait until you got home to play the tape back on your own personal television set and VCR.

Measuring Device

This is optional, as anyone can measure a dog with a yardstick and a straightedge. But the ACME Measurer™ used by most Flyball judges is made especially for measuring dogs. You can order one from the ACME Machine Company, 2901 Fremont Ave. South, Minneapolis, MN 55408. The phone number is (612) 827-3571.

Two-way Radio Headsets

With all of the noise at a Flyball tournament, it is beneficial to have direct communication between the captain and the box loader. During a race, if you need to communicate anything to the person at the box, you can scream as loud as you want and all you'll do is lose your voice. Box

Two-way radio headsets allow the captain to communicate with the box loader in spite of the noise of the Flyball racing. The headsets can also be used by someone in the racing area to communicate with team members in the crating area, to let them know they will be racing soon.

loaders can only see your lips moving (that's if you're able to get their attention).

There is a two-way radio headset available that allows communication between two people in a noisy environment. They were originally used by motorcyclists and called bike-to-bike mikes. They are now available at Radio Shack stores for around $100. This is fairly reasonable for radio headsets, and in the future I see these being a necessity for all teams. You may ask, "What kinds of things do you need to tell your box loader?" Actually, box loaders need to know things like: "Don't touch the box! Stand in front of it so that the box judge knows there's a malfunction," or, "The little dog is running fourth this time," or "Load a fifth ball in the gosh-darned box!" There are many different reasons why you need to communicate with your box loader.

Starting Lights (Electronic Judging System)

This is definitely optional. At $4,000 a set, most teams feel they can do without their own lights. However, our team has at least talked about doing this, and while it might seem crazy in 1997, it could be standard equipment for most teams ten years from now. Who knows? The lights are expensive because of the electronic components and the laser beams and sensors. If the cost of these electronic items were to go down substantially, it could place purchasing individual timing light systems within reach of many teams.

The Electronic Judging System (EJS) consists of timing lights, laser beam sensors (at the start/finish line) and a digital time clock (at the head table).

Collar

A semi-choke or buckle collar is best for Flyball training. Premier™ Pet Products manufactures two excellent Flyball collars. One is a semi-choke collar, which slides on over the dog's head and will tighten enough to prevent the dog from pulling out of it, but will not tighten enough to choke the dog. The other is the Premier Collar™, which is a martingale type of collar, which also slips on over the dog's head and lies flat. But when held by the loop part, this collar will tighten enough to prevent the dog from slipping out, but will not choke. I like either of these collars because the loops lie flat when not in use, and the dog cannot put his foot through the loop and injure himself.

Premier Pet Products
2406 Krossridge Road
Richmond, VA 23236
Phone (800) 933-5595

Another type that is popular amoung Flyball enthusiasts is a buckle collar with a permanent loop, which forms a handle, sewn to the collar. The loop sticks out so that it is easy to grab when you are catching your dog. There are various suppliers of this type of collar, which is sold under various names. Below is the address for the FX Pro™ VIPER collar.

Pet Safety Products
P.O. Box 475
Sparta, NJ 07871-0475
Phone (800) 448-4256

Harness

There are various types of harnesses available. The Premier Pet Products company (see collar section) manufactures a good, adjustable, nonrestrictive type harness, which you can get in a variety of colors to match your Flyball collar. The important consideration when choosing a harness is that it be nonrestrictive. A "V" neck is preferred to a harness with a horizontal breast strap going across the dog's chest above the front legs. The harness should also be well-fitting, and not have any dangling parts that could trip the dog or get caught in something.

Leashes

Several types of leashes are useful in Flyball training and competition. Retractable leads, like the Flexi™ Lead are useful, as well as 6-foot leashes, long lines and shorter traffic leads.

Miscellaneous Gear

In addition, you may need some of the following items for training or competition:

- Turning board—used to correct a wide turn off the box.

- Traffic cone—used to correct a bad turn off the box.

- Clipboards—to hold your statistic sheets.

- Statistic forms—for keeping records at practice and tournaments.

- Water and bowls—Flyball dogs get hot and thirsty.

- Motivational toys (target)—the main motivation for the dog.

- Clean-up kit (scoop, plastic bags and receptacle)—don't leave home without it!

- Treats—positive reinforcers.

- Clicker—for shaping the various parts of Flyball racing.

- Snow fence or ring gates—for lining the jumps to correct a problem.

- Fence stakes—to hold up the snow fence outdoors.

- Throw can—for correcting bad behavior.

- Vet Wrap—for protecting the dog's carpal pads.

- Towels—for wiping sand or dirt off the balls.

- Wading pool—for hot summer practices or competition.

This Whippet is wearing a customized harness with extra padding which cushions her body when she strains and jumps repeatedly four feet off the ground in anticipation of flyball racing.

These quick and easy-to-build Flyball jumps require no fasteners and they lie flat for storage. *Joanne Weber*

Chapter 3

Equipment
Construction

How to Build the Jumps

Materials needed: one sheet of plywood ($^3/_8$" to $^3/_4$" depending on your preference)

There are many ways to build a set of Flyball jumps. By far the easiest to build, store, and use at tournaments are what I call the "quick and easy" Flyball jumps. They can be cut out from one sheet of 4-foot by 8-foot plywood and do not require any fastening with glue, nails or screws to hold them together!

The uprights are essentially elongated triangles. The height of each upright measures 24 inches and the base of each upright is 16 inches high. There is a circular hole (for ease of carrying and storing) at the top of the uprights.

The top point of the triangle is rounded off to ensure safety. In the center of each upright there is a vertical slot measuring $12^1/_2$ inches. The slot begins 4 inches from the base, which rests on the floor, and goes up to a height of $16^1/_2$ inches above the floor. This will accommodate all of the boards necessary to achieve the maximum jump height of 16 inches. The extra $^1/_2$ inch makes it possible to get those boards in and out easily. The width of the slot should be slightly bigger than the width of the plywood you are using for the baseboard. The uprights can be no shorter than 24 inches and no taller than 36 inches. Most clubs use the 24-inch height.

The base board for each jump measures 8 inches by 32 inches. There is a 4-inch high vertical slot cut into the bottom of each of the 8-inch

By cutting the holes in exactly the same place at the top of each upright, handling is made easy, and you will avoid pinched fingers. *Joanne Weber*

boards. This slot is as wide as the plywood you will be using for uprights. In other words, if you are using $^1/_2$-inch plywood, make the slot just a hair bigger than $^1/_2$ inch wide. The edge of the slot would be just about 3 $^1/_2$ inches in from either end of the board so that the measurement of jump spanning between each upright is 24 inches.

The various upright boards are cut to the necessary sizes (1 inch by 32 inches, 2 inches by 32 inches and 4 inches by 32 inches). You can use less than a 32-inch length for these as they only need to be long enough to stick out on either side of the slots, which are about 25 inches apart (depending on the width of your plywood).

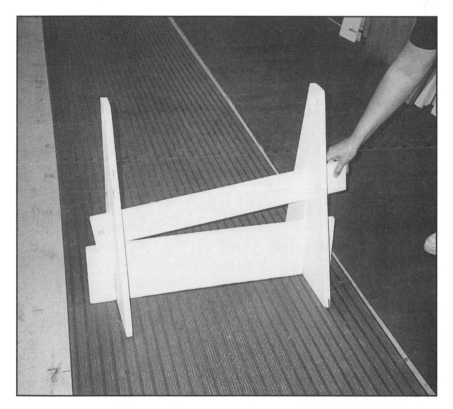

Extra boards just slide into the slots to raise the jump height. The base board is the minimum jump height of 8 inches. They can be quickly added or taken out between heats at a tournament. *Joanne Weber*

A length of 30 inches, 28 inches or even 26 inches is sufficient, although it looks nicer if all your boards are the same length. You will need enough height boards to make each jump 16 inches high for a tournament. A 4-inch, a 2-inch and two 1-inch boards for each jump will be needed. It is a good idea to have spare 1 and 2-inch boards handy in case they are broken during a race.

After cutting out the pieces (a base and two uprights per jump), all you have to do is fit them together and you have a basic 8-inch Flyball jump. The additional boards slide through the slots in the uprights to raise and lower the jump heights.

The jump bases and boards should be painted a dull, flat white. The size of each board can be stenciled on the ends of the boards (1-, 2-, 3- and 4-inch). This is especially helpful if you use 3-, 5- or 6-inch boards as many people can't tell the size by looking at it. Most host clubs only bother with the 1- , 2- and 4-inch boards, and mark the board size to avoid confusion.

The uprights may be painted white or any other color, or they can be decorated with your club or sponsor's logo or advertisement. You may also put a small logo on each of the white 8-inch base boards, provided you maintain a 2-inch white border around the edges.

When you have the jumps built, you can hang them from a peg on the wall for easy storage, or lie them flat.

What width of plywood you use depends on whether you want heavy-duty jumps or highly portable jumps. My original set is made from $3/4$-inch plywood and is quite sturdy. The subsequent sets I have built are made from $3/8$-inch or $1/2$-inch plywood, and they are rugged enough for my dogs. They are lightweight and portable, and don't take up much room. We have also started using these sets at tournaments as the boards are lighter and a dog is less likely to injure himself if he accidentally breaks one of the boards.

Lonnie's Quick and Easy Puppy Jumps

Baby jumps can be built for teaching stride length to puppies by cutting a slot in eight pieces of plywood. You could also use a piece of 2-inch by 6-inch lumber, cut into pieces at least 6 inches long.

Materials needed: scrap lumber or plywood pieces, at least 6" square

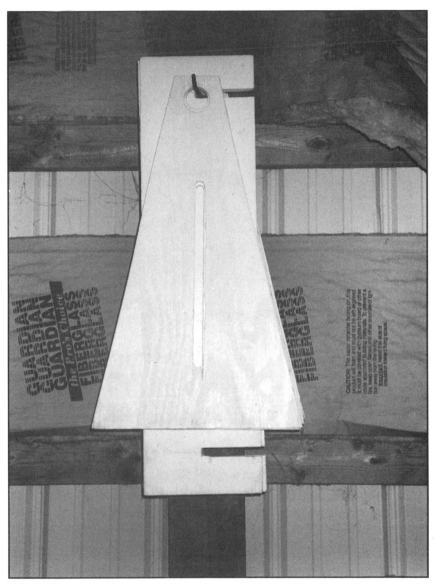

The jumps can be stored out of the way by hanging them on the wall. *Joanne Weber*

Take any thickness of plywood and cut a slot the width of the boards you intend to use. The slot needs only to be high enough for a 4-inch board, at the most, so the piece of plywood you use could measure as small as 6 inches by 6 inches.

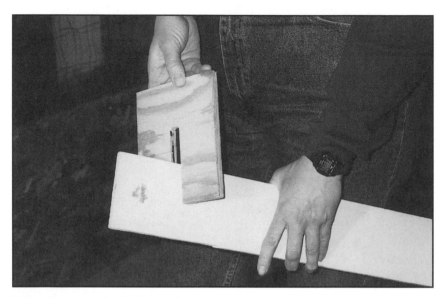

Puppy jumps don't need to be fancy. They are just blocks of wood which can be used to hold up a 1", 2", 3" or 4" board. *Joanne Weber*

Simply slide the slotted squares of wood over either end of a 1-, 2- or 4-inch board. Sometimes they fall over with the 1-inch boards in them, so I often just lay them flat with the 1-inch boards sticking into the slots.

Lightweight, Portable Backstop

Materials needed: 15 pieces $\frac{1}{2}$" PVC pipe (10 foot sections); 50' of snow fence (the kind of plastic snow fence that has holes small enough to prevent the smallest balls from getting through); 12 grommet bungies; 24 $\frac{1}{2}$" PVC elbow joints; 12 $\frac{1}{2}$" PVC "T" joints; 6 end caps for $\frac{1}{2}$" PVC pipe; 1 package of zippy ties.

Many clubs have backstops that are made of plywood or fiberboard and are quite heavy and unwieldy to transport. Being a veteran tournament director since the early days and having fought with every type of backstop imaginable, I designed one that can be carried by one person, in one hand, and does not require a rocket scientist to understand how to get parts A and B together!

Get some sharp scissors and cut the length of your 4-foot-high snow fence into two 2-foot-high sections. The backstop will require only one

This puppy got an early taste of Flyball training. At the end of the five-day camp in Japan, we had "show-off" day. This puppy could do single hops between the jumps (set about one meter apart) and go take a treat off the box pedal.

of these sections, but keep the other one around—you can always use it to make chutes to line the jumps. If you think you will be hosting a two-ring tournament, it would be a good idea to use the other 50-foot section to build a second backstop.

Cut your PVC pipe into the following lengths:

- 12 pieces at 59 inches

- 12 pieces at 47 inches

- 18 pieces at 24 inches

- 6 pieces at 10 inches

- 3 pieces at 2 inches

Cut your snow fence material into the following lengths:

- 3 pieces at 10 feet

- 3 pieces at 8 feet

This lightweight and portable backstop can be used on rings with 10 feet between racing lanes or 20 feet between racing lanes.

Arrange your PVC pipe so that you make "double rectangles," which look like an elongated digital number "8," using four of the 59-inch pieces and three of the 24-inch pieces. Use the elbow connectors on the four outer corners and use two "T" connectors to connect the 59-inch pieces with each other; join them with the 24-inch piece that goes in the center to give more support to the structure.

Cut a 10-foot section of snow fence and place it over the frame you have just made from PVC pipe. Attach it to the PVC pipe every few feet with plastic "zip tie" fasteners. If 10 feet comes at an odd place on your snow fence, trim it down to the next smaller measurement that is completely enclosed by the mesh squares. Cut off any extra plastic along the edges that does not make a complete square. Make two more of these 10-foot sections of backstop.

This lightweight, modular backstop can be carried in one hand. It is held together with grommet bungies.

Construct the 8-foot sections for the side and center panels of your backstop using four 47-inch pieces of PVC pipe and three 24-inch pieces of PVC pipe for each panel. In the same manner as for the larger sections already constructed, connect your PVC pipe to make the double rectangle, using a "T" joint in one lower corner of each panel instead of an elbow. This "T" will form the 90-degree angle to complete the rectangular frame, and will have a place to attach a small 2-inch connector, which will join with another "T" joint. Two 10-inch pieces will come out of either side of the straight part of the second "T," forming a base that will hold the free ends of the backstop upright. Place end caps on the exposed ends of the 10-inch pieces. Cut your 8-foot lengths of snow fence and attach them to the three panels you have constructed.

A grommet bungie is a 4- to 5-inch-long bungie cord that makes a loop. It has a marble at one end—like a child's ponytail holder. Using two grommet bungies, connect one of the 8-foot panels to the center support of one of your 10-foot panels, forming a "T" shape (connect the end of the 8-foot panel that does not have the "foot" support). Connect another 10-foot section to either side of the first one, using two bungies at each connecting point. Connect the two remaining 8-foot sections to the ends of the 10-foot sections, forming "L" shapes on each end. When constructed, you should have a structure that looks a lot like a gigantic letter "E."

The back of the backstop measures 30 feet across. This will accommodate racing lanes which are set 20 feet apart, with 5 feet on either side of the lane. If you have your lanes set up 10 feet apart, you can attach the 8-foot side panels to the center supports of the 10-foot end panels, making the inside dimensions of the backstop 20 feet wide.

How to Build a Flyball Box

The directions that follow are very general ones for a basic, wedge-style box with a full-face pedal. This is the type of box that would be good for training beginner dogs. This box could also be used in competition, but I strongly urge anyone who wishes to get serious about the sport to consider purchasing a commercially made box.

Materials needed: 1 sheet of $^1/_2$" plywood ($^3/_4$" can be used for more stability, $^3/_8$" can be used for lighter weight); 2' by

2' square of rubber matting; 2' section of piano hinge; a hook and latch; 2 expansion springs ($3/4$" by 3" light tension); 2 helical springs ($1/2$" by 2"); several small eye bolts; 1 piece of wood, 4" by 16"; $1/2$" wood screws; 1" wood screws; scrap pieces of 2" by 4"; $1/2$" thick foam rubber, 24" square; scrap pieces of 2" by 2" for corner supports.

The Base

Cut the floor (base) of your box from your plywood. The length of your floor can vary, but needs to be only 24 inches to 28 inches long. Your box can be up to 24 inches wide. Most competition boxes are 20 inches to 22 inches wide. You can make yours smaller for easier transport if you prefer.

The Sides

The configuration of the sides of your box depends on the angle you desire on your pedal. On a 45-degree-angle box, the length of the slope would be 26 inches. You can get the angle on your box by using a protractor and drawing a line at the degree of the angle you want, then cutting the board. The triangular shape that makes up the height, base and slope of the pedal is a right triangle. The formula for a right triangle is A squared + B squared = C squared. Side A is the height (18 inches), side B is the base (19 inches). The squares of A (324) and B (361) add up to 685. The square root of 685 is 26.17, so the pedal side will be a little over 26 inches long. The box I built of my own design has a 70-degree angle on the pedal. This means that on an 18-inch-tall box, the length of the slope would be $19^1/_2$ inches, but the base would only be $7^1/_2$ inches. To add more stability to this box, I did not make the sides triangular, but extended the box another 14 inches back, creating a side view more like a trapezoid.

The Pedal

Cut your pedal to match the width of your baseboard, and to match the length of the angle on your side boards. A steeper angle will require a shorter pedal. A 45-degree-angle pedal will need a piece of wood 26 inches long by 20 inches wide; a 70-degree-angle box will need a pedal $19^1/_2$ inches tall by 20 inches wide. Note that no matter what dimensions or angles you use, from the dog's perspective, he still sees a box, 18 inches tall and 20 inches wide with the center of the cup 13 inches from the floor.

Note the different angles on the pedals of the boxes in front, and the resulting shapes of the side pieces. The wedge-shaped box on the left is a better box for training beginners. The more upright box on the right is made for dogs who will bank off the box with their turn. Notice it is more heavily padded than the one on the left. When fast dogs hit the box on the left, they want to go upwards because there's nothing to stop them. *Joanne Weber*

The Backboard

Cut the backboard to fit between the side boards. If you have a box that is 20 inches wide, then the backboard must be 20 inches wide, less the width of your plywood sides. If you are using $1/2$-inch plywood and have a 20-inch base, the backboard will be 19 inches wide. Your box cannot be more than 18 inches tall, so the height of your backboard must be no greater than 18 inches, less the width of your plywood making up the base and the top (17 inches, if you are using $1/2$-inch plywood). This board will basically be 17 inches tall by 20 inches wide, with cutouts made along the bottom for the loader to place his feet into so that he may lean into the back of the box with his shins. The holes can be cut right out of the corners, and need to be about 6 inches square. Because the loader does a lot of leaning into the box with his shins, it is nice to attach a few inches of foam, enclosed in vinyl or some other upholstery material to the backboard. If you don't want to get that fancy, you can just attach a foam kneeling pad, for use in gardening, to the back of the box. Be sure to leave room for cocking the hammer on the box if this is the kind of propulsion you will be using.

The Top Board

The top board (triangular boxes do not have a top board) needs to be as wide as the base and the pedal, and will go over the side boards. The best way to attach the top to the sides (and the bottom to the sides) is to use a piece of 2-inch by 2-inch (which really only measures $1^1/_2$ inches by $1^1/_2$ inches) in the corners. Screw the top (and the bottom) board into the side pieces, and also into the 2 by 2, for extra support. Put additional screws in from the sides and into the 2 by 2. The backboard will provide additional support to the top and sides that enclose it.

Where the 2 by 2 reinforcements reach the front of the box, cut them at the same angle as the face of the box. If your hinge is at the bottom, then at the top you should drill a hole ($^1/_2$ inch to $^5/_8$ inch) into each 2 by 2 to insert a small helical spring, which will keep the pedal off the latch release until triggered. Drill the hole to fit the length of your spring, leaving enough spring as needed exposed to support the pedal. Note that on the triangular-shaped box, there will be no room at the top for this spring, so you can move it further down on each side.

The Hinge

Decide if you want your hinge at the top of the pedal or the bottom. Most dogs hit the bottom half of the pedal when they trigger the box. Little dogs don't have to be as high or hit as hard if the hinge is at the top of the box. However, most competition boxes in use have the hinge at the bottom. The box is easier to open up for fixing mechanical problems with the hinge at the bottom. On the box I designed, I put the hinge at the top. Actually, on the first box I designed, I did not use a hinge at all. The pedal moved straight out and back on nylon drawer rollers, which I thought was a very efficient setup, considering the direction of the impact and the fact that all dogs do not hit the pedal in the same place. I have never seen a similar system in anyone else's box design, however. Everyone commonly uses hinges.

The Ball Cup

The center of the hole for the ball cup should be approximately 13 inches from the ground. You can decide for yourself whether to center the hole or offset it to the right or left (which some teams have done to aid their dogs in turning). The hole must be big enough to accommodate a tennis

Wooden corner reinforcements help make the box sturdier and are a good place to put springs.

ball. You can saw a hole in the plywood and bevel the edge so there will be no sharp edges, or you can line it with a plastic (PVC) cuff that measures $2^7/_8$ inches inside diameter (3 inches outside diameter).

The cuff makes the cup smooth and makes the hole look close to perfectly round. The cuff needs to be only $1^3/_4$ inches long, and you will have to cut out a section on the inside of the box to allow for the hammer arm to come up and swat the ball out of the cup. If you do not use the plastic cuff, you will need some form of chute to keep the ball from falling into the Flyball box when you load it.

You can make a ball enclosure from two blocks of wood that are 5 inches long, 2 inches wide and 2 inches thick. Cut half-moon shapes into the edges of each piece. A tennis ball is $2^1/_2$ inches in diameter, so the chute should be about 3 inches in diameter. The hammer is going to come through the center, so your chute has to be in two pieces, one on either side of the hammer. Position the chute pieces on the under side of the pedal, where they will not impede the movement of the hammer arm.

Rubber Matting

You can pad the front of the pedal with foam rubber, or you can attach the rubber matting directly to the plywood. Bring the rubber matting around the edges and staple it to the back of the pedal. Cut and tuck the spare material around the corners so that it looks nicer and does not form a big wad of mat at each corner. You can attach the hinge over the rubber matting (if you keep it smooth) on the back of the pedal, or you can choose to bring the matting only to the edge on the side (top or bottom) which will have the hinge, then staple the mat right to the edge of the $^1/_2$-inch plywood pedal. Matting has ridges. Most people have the ridges of the matting going side-to-side (horizontally) to help the dog slow down and get traction for leaving the box. There is the line of thinking, however, which says the 70-degree-angle box pedal helps to stop the dog, and traction is needed for turning sideways, which would mean you would want your ridges going up and down (vertically) if you're using mats with ridges.

Propulsion Systems

The propulsion mechanism is the most important part of the box. There are many designs for projecting the ball into the air. The variety is limited only by the imagination. I have seen setups using door latches, pistons, bungie cords, all sorts of things. The propulsion device (mechanism) in the box I built for my team was engineered by a man in Michigan. It involves a piston-type, spring-loaded cup. It functions somewhat like a dart gun. This unit can be put into a box with a stationary cup, or a cup

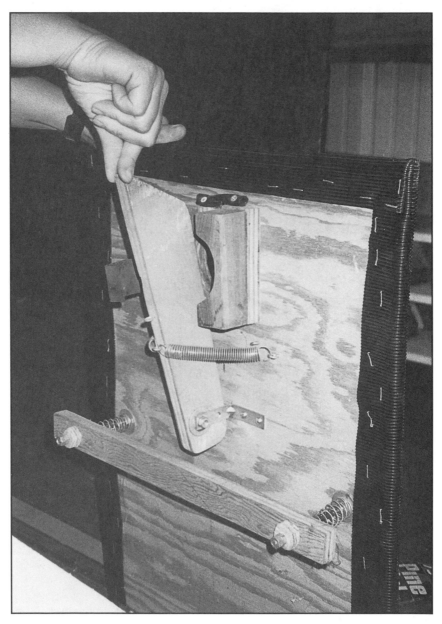

The hammer arm assembly. This one is attached to the underside of the pedal. Note that there is no actual cup; the ball just rests on the hammer when it is in the chute.

that moves with the pedal. It can be removed and replaced with another in the event of a malfunction.

The whole unit is self-contained, and there are no latches to wear out or keep aligned. It's pretty spiffy, but plans cannot be included for it as the engineer is currently seeking a patent on the unit. I encourage people to keep imagining ways to come up with a "better mousetrap." The only limitation on design is that the triggering mechanism *cannot* be *electronic*. Keep in mind that the ball must go into the air and fly without obstruction for at least 24 inches in the direction of the start/finish line.

Another thing to think about when designing a propulsion device is that the faster the box reacts and the faster the ball comes out, the faster the dog can turn and run with the ball. One time, when our team switched to a new box, the triggering mechanism was a hair slower than it had been on our previous box, and the faster dogs turned around without the ball. They didn't wait for it. This was a valuable experience. It taught us that the dogs have the turn and run down pat, and that they will turn around regardless of how fast the ball is tossed. If faster balls lead to faster turns, then we have to come up with an even faster triggering mechanism.

For a basic, hammer-style propulsion system, you will need:

- a hammer (throwing arm) which can be made of plywood, hardwood, tubular (1-inch square) aluminum or anything else that will work

- a spring latch and catch system

- some springs; a hinge; and a piece of metal or other material to make contact with the latch when the pedal is depressed

Let's assume you're using a wooden arm (hammer). You can attach it to a hinge that is connected to the bottom of the box, or you can attach it right to the back of the pedal. The hinge can be a regular, triangular-shaped door hinge, or you can make your own by drilling a hole through the hammer at one end. Place a pin (carriage bolt) through this hole, which will support the hammer between two metal brackets, holding it onto the back of the pedal. Use a screw or bolt that will be flush with the outside front pedal, and attach the brackets with washers and nuts, rather than using wood screws from the underside of the box.

Make sure that any screws that are put into the back of the pedal do not protrude through to the front of the box, where the dogs' paws will be hitting. The bottom end of this hammer is rounded, so that it will swing away from the pedal without rubbing on the wood. The back (spine) of the hammer has a small eyebolt to attach two 3-inch to 4-inch expansion springs. The other ends of the two springs attach to the back of the pedal several inches to either side of (and slightly below) the cup. You can make the hammer faster or slower by using tighter springs, or by spreading the eyebolts further apart to put more tension on the springs.

In the back of the box you will have to cut a slot extending about 10 inches from the top edge. This slot must be wide enough to allow the hammer to move freely within it. It will help to make the sides of the slot very smooth by adding plastic coating or metal tape to the exposed sides of the slot. To one side of the slot, attach a block of wood—2 inches square is large enough.

If you want a more efficient releasing mechanism, you can bevel the corner of the block of wood to match the angle at which the hammer will be when it is cocked. Attach the spring latch to this block of wood with the hook facing the slot.

On the plywood hammer, attach the catch for the spring latch. You should experiment to find the best location for the latch and catch, considering the speed and strength of propulsion desired.

You will need a push bar attached to the back of the pedal to depress the release on the latch assembly. This consists of a flat piece of metal approximately 6 inches long and 1^1/$_2$ inches wide. The top edge is bent over about ^{1}/$_2$ inch from the edge and drilled so that two screws can hold it into place on the back of the pedal. The bottom edge is bent over (in the same direction) about ^{1}/$_2$ inch to form the latch release depressing surface. Situate this piece of metal on the box pedal so that when the pedal is depressed, the metal "foot" will come in contact with the latch release. This will cause the latch head to ease back off the catch, and the hammer will shoot the ball out of the cup. To make the box more "hairtrigger," you can bend the metal foot down to make contact with the latch release sooner. If the release is too hairtrigger, bend the metal back, so that it takes more than a slight bump to trigger the box.

The Finishing Touches

There are a number of things you can do to finish constructing your basic box.

Adding a coat of paint and your team's logo or other design will spruce up your box. Applying some non-skid surface material on the bottom of the box will give it more stability on rubber matting and grass.

Plastic carpet runner material, stapled to the bottom of the box, pointy-side-out, will keep your box from sliding. Anti-slip surfacing, sold for use on van and motor home steps, works well, too.

To muffle the noise that the Flyball box makes, line the front edge of the box sides (where the pedal meets the box) with some foam insulation tape. The hammer can be muffled by attaching a short (3-inch) section of soft rubber tubing above the cup where the hammer strikes the top of the pedal. Just put a short screw through either end of the tubing to hold it in place. Attaching handles will make the box easier to pick up and transport.

To keep the pedal from flopping open while lifting the box or during play, you can attach a small rope, leather strap or other (removable) safety strap that will allow the box to open only so far. The child-proof cupboard door locks work well for this type of latch; however, they do tend to break over time.

A ball tray, or bin, can be added to the back of the box so that the loader does not have to turn around to get more balls. Just make sure that none of the balls are visible from the front of the box.

Many other options, from retractable wheels to stabilizing stakes (for outdoor use) can be added to your box, depending on how much weight you are willing to add to a contraption that already weighs close to 40 pounds.

Some dogs like balls but don't know how to catch them. Bouncing the ball on the floor gives the dog a chance to grab the ball from the air. *Joanne Weber*

Chapter 4

Flyball Basics

Ball Work

If you already have a ball-crazy dog, you just need to teach him how to grab the ball and run with it. If your dog does not already retrieve the ball, you can shape the Retrieve by using something your dog enjoys as a reward, like food.

If your dog will not catch the ball, start out by bouncing the ball. Then, as you see the dog trying to catch the ball, lob short little tosses. As catching skill increases, throw the ball harder, and encourage your dog to reach for it. Make it increasingly challenging. Try to see if you can throw the ball past the dog without him snatching it. This will develop catching prowess. See the section on catching in Chapter 11 .

The "snatch and run" can be practiced separately with a ball, a flexi-leash and your dog. Place the ball on the ground about 15 feet away from you (within the range of your flexi-leash). As the dog picks up the ball, lock the flexi-leash and give a firm jerk as you call the dog's name. This teaches "get it and go!" No lollygagging at the box! As soon as your dog has the ball, he must turn and run. The dog must learn to spin around and race to you at the sound of his name.

Shaping the Retrieve

Some dogs need to be taught to like the ball. The easiest way I have found to do this is to "shape" the Retrieve. I developed this method in 1989 when faced with the dilemma of teaching my Welsh Corgi puppy to retrieve. She wasn't showing interest in the ball, and I didn't want to use the ear pinch. I needed a method that was going to produce a fail-safe Retrieve.

My method puts together a combination of techniques that are commonly used in animal training to create a new method by using the techniques in a way that I had never seen or heard of before. The method incorporates positive reinforcement, shaping and backward chaining. Shaping uses strictly positive reinforcement and no force or corrections. This method works well on any food-motivated dog.

How It Works

First, define the exercise for the dog. This is something I always do before training. I have to sit down and put myself in the dog's place and decide what is really ultimately being asked of the dog. I decided that this exercise would be called, "put it in my hand." The command would be, Get It!

Start at the end of the exercise. I started with my puppy, "Weasel," spitting out the ball into my hand on the command Thank-You. Someone might have invented this method a lot sooner except for the irony of asking the dog to spit out something she has not yet learned to take. If my method seems backwards, that's because it is! Remember, it's a backward chain, beginning at the end.

Each time Weasel spit the ball into my hand on the cue, she received a treat and praise. It doesn't matter how the ball goes into the mouth, *as long as no discomfort or stress is involved.* Just reward for the release of the ball, which is the last part of the behavior chain. I would sneak the ball into Weasel's mouth, then quickly say, "Thank-You" and give her a treat for complying (spitting the ball into my waiting hand).

The next link in the chain is the Hold It part. With Weasel, there was some mild difficulty involved in getting her to keep the ball in her mouth at first. Starting with just an instant and increasing the requirement gradually to seconds, I helped hold the ball in her mouth with my fingers on her muzzle. I praised her for this new accomplishment and said, "Good Hold It." She knew that "good" was a positive reinforcer that meant a treat was coming. After the Thank-You command and her releasing the ball to my hand, she got her treat and more praise.

Teaching the dog a quick ball pickup should be done away from the box to avoid any negative association. As soon as the dog has the ball, the dog's name is shouted, the leash is jerked and the owner runs in the opposite direction.

The last link of the behavior chain is the Take It command. For this, I used the phrase, Get It. This would seem to be the hardest part of training—to get the dog to voluntarily grab the ball without any use of force. It was made simple with the use of shaping (rewarding the dog for each successive approximation). I worked on this separately, without the Hold or Release. I held the ball in one hand and a treat and a clicker in the other. The dog had been conditioned to the clicker and understood its meaning to be, "Great job, you've earned a treat!"

At first, if Weasel even bumped the ball with her nose, I would give a reward (click and treat). Then, when she opened her mouth slightly, I rewarded that. Finally, the dog had to put her mouth around the ball to get a reward. This progressed rather quickly, and after a few repetitions, my dog was grabbing the ball with gusto. Then, I "named" the behavior. It's important not to use the words, "Get it!" until the dog is actually performing the exercise. You don't want him to think that the command, Get

"Weasel" (U-Agl, U-CD Gelert's Wascally Weasel, FM, DSA) knows she can trade in a ball for one treat. Weasel is owned by the author. She is the number one Pembroke Welsh Corgi in the sport of Flyball (most points earned). She runs the course in 6.1 seconds, which is quite good for a dog of this breed! *Joanne Weber*

It means to sit there with your mouth clamped shut, refusing to take the ball. Be sure to always pair the command with the completed action you will expect to receive from the dog when you give that command.

I then added the remaining links in the behavior chain: the hold and release to my hand. Weasel's progress was phenomenal! She seemed to grasp very quickly that she couldn't perform the last part of the exercise (release it to my hand) without performing the first part (take the ball). The Hold became automatic, as it was sandwiched between the Take and the Release. She would not get rewarded for dropping the ball prematurely, for example, on the ground. The reward only followed the successful completion of the last link in the chain: drop it into my hand on command.

The next stage of Retrieve training is to make the dog reach for the ball. I had to try to get Weasel to pick up the ball from the ground. This involved shaping the first three links to include:

1. lowering the hand with the ball by increments, gradually, to the ground

2. requiring longer holds

3. requiring delivery to hand every time

Finally, the dog must perform a pick-up from the ground or other surface. Weasel did it accidentally while I was watching television. I was taking a break from training, and she became impatient. Weasel figured that the ball was legal tender with a value of one treat. While I was not paying attention, she picked up the ball from my lap and was trying desperately to give it to me. She was trying to cash it in for a treat! Now all I had to do was to place the ball farther and farther away from me. This incorporated the Go Out for the Retrieve and also a longer Hold. A Sit Front can also be added here. Weasel added it on her own, as she would bring the ball in and look up for her treat. If at any point she lost interest while bringing the ball back, or dropped it before I asked for it, I would say, "Get it—where's your ball?" There was no reward until she put the ball right into my hand *on command*.

Soon, I was able to throw the ball out and say, "Get it," and Weasel would dash out and do a great Retrieve. (When I say "soon," I mean later in the afternoon of the same day we began the very first step.) This method is not only successful, it's fast!

was not a retriever and as a puppy was not at all interested in the ball. In one short afternoon, I ended up with a dog who would take a ball on command and hold it until asked to give it up. I then had a dog who would run for the ball and run back, and would sit before relinquishing the ball to my hand. I was very satisfied. I achieved the same quick results that I had previously achieved using the ear pinch method without causing any distress to my little puppy. I have since used this method on other dogs with much success.

Box Work

When introducing the Flyball box, begin by familiarizing your dog with the box while it is uncocked and unloaded. Praise your dog for going near it. Use a reassuring and calm tone of voice to encourage him. Loading the box can be a frightening experience, causing your dog to avoid it. When the dog will approach the box without a problem, you can begin shaping the pedal push.

Shaping the Flyball Box Pedal Push

Shaping is defined as teaching something in graduated steps. In the beginning, you reward the dog for performing every attempt towards the action that you want. Then, you can gradually begin requiring closer approximations to what you are trying to achieve. As you reward each successive step, stop rewarding previous levels of achievement until the dog is doing exactly what is required. For more information on shaping, I suggest you read *Don't Shoot the Dog*, by Karen Pryor.

When working the box, the first rule is to always keep at least two spare balls in your hands at all times. This way, if your dog misses the first ball that is tossed or propelled from the box, you will always have a spare so that the dog can receive positive reinforcement for performing correctly.

Encourage your dog to make physical contact with the box. Use the ball as a lure, and when the dog accidentally touches the box, reward him with praise *and* the ball. (Praise is "Good hit it.")

When the dog shows no qualms about touching the box, proceed to reward only touches on the pedal area of the box. Reward this action with praise and toss the ball for the dog. Ignore all other attempts in which the dog does not make contact with the pedal. Never put a ball in the cup at this stage, or you will have a dog bent on prying the ball out of

When Weasel was a puppy, her box was introduced as a food table. She would come running in from outdoors, dash to the living room and climb up on the box looking for a snack!

the hole with her nose instead of using a paw to trigger the pedal, as it should be done. When the dog hits the pedal area the majority of the time, begin rewarding only direct hits that are strong enough to trigger the box.

After the dog walks up and slaps the pedal with his foot, you can start cocking the box, which will make a thumping noise when the pedal is hit. Do not load the box at this time, just cock it. Get your dog used to the sound. Toss a ball to the dog and use praise as a reward for hitting the pedal.

Start working with two people, if you haven't already. The handler needs to walk the dog up to the box, with the helper tossing balls to the dog as a reward. When the dog catches the ball tossed by the helper, the handler calls the dog's name, then turns and runs with the dog.

When the dog ignores (or positively associates) the sound of the box, begin loading it too. Lure your dog up to the box, as always, with the *other* ball. When the dog hits the pedal, be ready to toss the other ball, as he may not see the one being projected out of the box. Always be prepared with an extra ball in each hand in case your dog misses the loaded one. The ball is the positive reinforcement. You want to make sure the dog

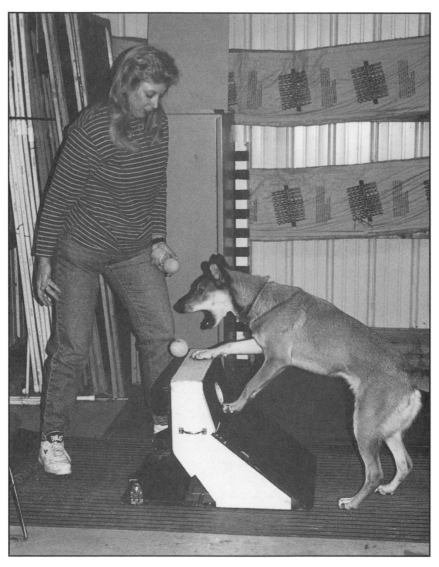

When working with a new dog, the helper should always keep a spare ball in each hand. If the dog makes a sudden leap of understanding, or accidentally does something right, you don't want to be caught empty-handed and unable to reward the dog. *Joanne Weber*

gets it every time. Once the ball is caught, call your dog's name, turn and run away (get the jumps out of the way—we're just working on the box, now).

Next, as the dog approaches the box and hits the pedal, the loader must hide the other ball behind the box so that the only ball in view is the

The loader lures the dog to the box, as usual, but this time, the box is loaded in the hope that the dog will get the ball about to fly out of the cup. *Joanne Weber*

one in the cup. If the first ball is missed, encourage the dog to get it and make sure the loader is prepared to throw a back-up ball. When the ball is caught, the handler calls the dog's name, turns and runs.

The loader lures the dog to the box, but hides the ball at the last instant. *Joanne Weber*

When the dog comprehends hitting the box and catching the ball from the cup, concentrate on the turn from the box. The instant the ball is caught, the handler calls the dog's name, and the dog should turn and run to (or with) the handler. If these turns are really slow, you can try giving a leash correction, but I definitely do not recommend any negative associations with the Flyball box. So, if you want to send the dog to re-trieve a ball placed on the floor in another part of the building, these steps would be better: say the name, jerk the leash, turn and run (to teach the "get it and GO").

Another thing you can do to produce quick turns at the box is to bounce a ball off the face of the box as your dog approaches. The dog will jump after the ball, landing on the pedal, but at about that time, the ball will have already bounced and be on its way back toward the finish line. The dog will have to hit and shove off the box virtually at the same in-stant, like a swimmer's turn, to leap after the ball. Your timing and angle of trajectory with the ball bounce must be really good. The dog actually is turning and catching the ball at the same time.

Teaching the Pedal Push with the Ricochet Method

If your dog has mastered the jumps, down and back, and is good at catch-ing a bounced ball, you can add the box at this point without separate box lessons. Send the dog down to a person bouncing a ball right in front of the box. Just as the dog gets to the ball, the person should bounce the ball so that it will be about 13 inches off the ground immediately in front of the pedal at the time the dog tries to catch it. Chances are the dog will leap for the ball, catch it while landing on the pedal, and of course, turn and run (because you will be calling). The idea here is to get the dog to use the box face as a landing pad/turning point.

When the dog is consistently landing on the pedal to catch the bounced ball, have the helper begin loading the box. When the dog lands on the box, there will be two balls flying—one from the cup and one bounced by the helper. As the dog starts noticing the one coming from the cup, have the helper begin hiding the bouncing ball just an instant before the dog lands on the pedal. The timing has to be perfect. If the loader hides the bouncing ball too soon, a dog may put on the brakes and not continue to run at the box. If the timing is right, the dog will land on the pedal, find the ball (sometimes after being hit in the chest or legs) and pick it up. Eventually, the dog will be looking for the ball in the cup and waiting to scoop the ball up as soon as it emerges. The loader should always keep the extra ball handy in case the dog misses the loaded ball. It is important that the dog get rewarded for hitting the pedal.

We have several dogs on our team who have learned the box in this manner. They never had any other kind of introduction to the box. They just started banking off of it when catching the bounced ball. Dogs who learn in this way have a much faster turn than those who think the box is a pedal that needs to be pressed.

However, some dogs just won't barrel down to the ball fast enough to run into the box, and some dogs are too "dainty" to put their feet on the box, and screech to a halt rather than land on it. For these dogs, you will have to go back to the pedal push shaping exercises.

The loader bounces the ball in front of the box, so that it reaches a height of 13" about the time the dog gets ready to grab it. Ideally, the dog will jump for the ball, land on the box as he is catching the ball, turn and run back to the owner. *Joanne Weber*

Other Box Rules and Hints

Don't let your dog have a ball from the box unless you have sent the dog. This is the same rule for everyone, and dogs cannot be allowed to help themselves to a ball. If you are loading and someone else's dog sneaks down and tries to get the ball, cover the cup with your hand, or otherwise disarm the box, so that the dog will not be rewarded for disobedience.

When you are loading, never give the dog more than one ball per turn. Some dogs are greedy, and will stand there all day trying to get several balls from the box. Also, when at a tournament or a practice, never reload the box until the departing dog is well on the way back. If you load it too soon, the dog may learn to try to turn around to get a second ball because he can hear a ball being loaded into the cup. Don't tempt your dog.

Never send a dog down to an untended box. If a dog learns that the box will slide when it is hit, the dog will be afraid to hit it with any amount of force. If you are loading for someone, always step into the box and stand on it to stabilize it.

If your dog has a wide turn off the box, work with a retractable leash or use a turning board. The turning board is just a piece of plywood that is placed beside the box on the side your dog turns toward. Most dogs turn the same way each time they trigger the box. Determine whether your dog is a right-hand turner or a left-hand turner. Have the loader set out the turning board so that your dog can't go wide. A dog that goes wide runs the danger of being tempted to go around the fourth jump.

If your dog is "vacationing" at the box (taking too long to turn, or "munching" the ball once or twice before turning), work on a correction with a retractable leash. Dogs must learn to whip around instantly upon hearing their name and come racing to you with that ball.

The loader is using a turning board to discourage dogs from making wide turns off the box. The loader must know to which side each dog turns to properly set the board.

Box work needs to be practiced separately from jumping. No dog is ever so well trained that it will not benefit from a restrained send-away (no jumps, just 50 feet of mat and the box). Run with your dog to build excitement, or just do a send down and call back, but try to get the dog running flat out, as fast as possible toward the box, and zipping right back to you.

Remember that the ball in the cup can never become more important than the ball or target at the end of the race. A dog who thinks the prize comes from triggering the box will saunter back over the jumps with all of the enthusiasm of one who knows this prize will be taken away at the finish line. The dog who runs to the box quickly but returns slowly can be reminded where the real jackpot lies by being sent down to an unloaded box a few times.

Remember—the real reward is always at the finish.

Chapter 5

The Training Regimen

Backward Chaining

Backward behavior chaining is a term used to describe a type of training in which the last behavior in a chain is taught first. Flyball is not one simple exercise. It is a series of over 25 behaviors completed together, in a chain. The easiest way for the dog to learn a chained behavior such as Flyball, Agility or Obedience is to start at the end and move toward the beginning. This accomplishes two very important things:

1. The task becomes ever easier for the dog, instead of more difficult, as you add each new part of the behavior chain. Why? Because you're not adding anything new on the end. You always finish up with something the dog already knows how to do well. Your dog therefore feels successful after completing each chained sequence.

2. Each behavior becomes a "cue" for the behavior that follows it. For example, jumping the fourth jump is the cue to hit the box; hitting the box is the cue to catch the ball; catching the ball is the cue to turn and run, and so on.

Beginning at the End

The Target

The *reward* for the dog is always at the *end* of the chain. The end of the chain is when the dog has successfully run the course and brought back the ball. This behavior is being performed for a *reason*, a reward. The reward must serve as the *goal,* the *focus* and the *target.* The reward can be the other ball you will give at the end. Or it could be a toy, a treat, a game of tug of war or a wrestling match. Whatever it is, it must be there each and every time for the dog. If you train without a target, your dog will run without focus and may wander into the other lane, try to turn around and run back to get another ball from the box or chase after another dog. The dog must be absolutely riveted on the target.

What you use for your target, or motivator, will depend on your dog. Do you know what motivates your particular dog? Selecting the right motivation for your dog is very important.

Dogs have been bred from their wild ancestors to excel at specific tasks. Long ago, folks started selecting (or rejecting) their breeding animals based on the traits that they wanted to emphasize or eliminate. From the original tasks for survival, including all of the ones necessary to obtain food, one or two have been selectively bred for in each breed. Breeders throughout history have tried to emphasize the desirable traits required for the work their dogs needed to perform.

For the dog's wild ancestors, obtaining food required the tasks of locating prey and singling out one that was more vulnerable than the others, chasing, catching, killing, eating and bringing food home to the den for the puppies. These tasks have been selectively bred in for different breeds to give us the variety of canines we have today. The herding breeds love to chase and catch things, the terriers like to chase and kill things, the retrievers like to catch and bring things. Some breeds just like to eat!

You will probably find that your dog is motivated by one or more things mentioned above. Terriers for example, will love to have a chance to "attack" a ball on a rope and shake it or swing from it as you pull the other end. Border Collies may love to latch onto an object like prey, too, or may just want to have you throw another ball. A breed that does not have chasing or killing as part of the built-in job description may respond to eating as a motivator. Some dogs are powerfully motivated by food. It has been my experience, however, that the dogs that are the most serious about Flyball racing are the ones who can be motivated to chase, grab or "attack" something at the end of their run.

The Finish Line and Target

Have a helper hold your dog. Call the dog to you while you are positioned over and past the finish line. Show the target. When your dog reaches you, give the target as a reward. This is what we call a "restrained Recall." The helper should not let go until the dog is really psyched up. It helps if the handler gets very excited. Why should the dog get excited if the owner is standing there blandly saying the dog's name? Jump up and down, call excitedly and run. You are training this dog for a race, after all. A dog will show only as much enthusiasm for this as the owner does.

Remember, this is not Obedience training. Even if you have a dog who will do a Sit-Stay, do not be tempted to leave the dog on a Stay and then call his name. Part of the excitement for the dog is wanting to be let go, but being held back. Your dog should be trying hard to break loose from the helper. This "breaking loose" cannot be experienced by being left on a Sit-Stay. Also, you must teach the dog to run (not walk) to you on his name. Please don't say, "Sparkle, come." This is not the Obedience ring where we do not want the dog to anticipate the Recall. We *want* the dog to come on the name, and we will not be using any Obedience commands. As I constantly remind my new students, *there are no "stays" or "comes" in Flyball training.*

Your dog will not be confused in the Obedience ring if you do this. Trust me. It has to do with context. If you were sitting at the dinner table and said, "Alex, pass the salt," it would be the same tone of voice you would use in the Obedience ring when you say, "Sparkle, come." Why didn't Alex fly out of the chair and run over to you when you said his name at the dinner table? Because you were using the name as a prefix to a request. Now, suppose you and Alex are walking through a cave and you come upon an enraged Grizzly bear. You yell, "ALEXXXXXX!" In this context, it means "turn around and run like crazy!" Just as you do with human verbal interaction, you can use a dog's name to get attention, to precede a directive, or to mean "get over here right now!" Dogs can discern the difference just like people can.

Also, when calling your dog, do not stand in the middle of the runway, as though your dog was going to do a Recall with a front. When the dog starts to run, you should run away with the target, and away from the dog, or toss a ball down the runway. If you are just standing there, the dog will stop. This is *not* a formal Recall. You want the dog to run well *past* the finish line.

A helper holds a dog for the first step in Flyball training, a restrained Recall to the finish line for his target. *Joanne Weber*

JUMP NO. 1 + FINISH + TARGET

The next step is to have the helper hold your dog behind the first jump. For the sake of consistency, I will always refer to the jump closest to the finish line as jump number 1.

The dog is held behind jump no. 1 for a restrained Recall to the owner, who has the dog's target object. *Joanne Weber*

Walk away and go *over* the jump yourself. The dog is not stupid. If he sees you go around the object, your dog will, too. Show him the target. Call. Get excited. The helper should let go and aim the dog toward the first jump. If the dog fails to jump, he does *not* get the target.

The dog was being held behind jump no. 2. He is focused on his target, which the owner threw as soon as it was evident that the dog had committed to both jumps. *Joanne Weber*

Try again. Remember not to walk around the jump. You can make it impossible for the dog to go around the jumps by lining the runway with snow fence. If you buy a 50-foot roll of 4-foot-high fence and cut it in half lengthwise, you will have two sections 2 feet high with which to line the jumps. When the dog is doing one jump and the finish well, you can go on.

Jump No. 2 + Jump No. 1 + Finish + Target

Now the helper should hold the dog behind jump no. 2. You want the dog to learn to do a single stride (one hop) between each jump, so you should set the jumps as close together as is necessary for your dog to get only one pounce between jumps. A dog that is less than 13 inches high at the shoulders may never learn to single stride the jumps at 10 feet apart. Don't push the dog to do singles if he is not large enough to do it.

The dog is held behind jump no. 3. It is important to move back gradually once you are sure the dog understands the previous steps.

If you are training without the aid of a snow fence, don't be surprised if the dog jumps only one of the two jumps. After all, that is all that has been learned so far, right? The dog will often run around the no. 2 jump, only to jump the no. 1, or maybe jump no. 2 and run around no. 1. Your dog knows how to jump only one jump so far. Don't worry. Be patient. Remember to walk through (over) the jumps. And don't give the target as a reward unless the dog does both jumps. When he is doing well repeatedly, go on.

Jump No. 3 + Jump No. 2 + Jump No. 1 + Finish + Target

If you are progressing slowly enough, a focused dog should have no trouble adding the third jump. Remember to space the jumps an equal distance apart. When your dog is doing well repeatedly, add the fourth jump.

Before moving on to the next step, the dog should be doing all four jumps with a single bounce between. With this particular dog, it took a while to stretch him out to be able to do singles (he's only 14" tall). We started with the jumps 8 feet apart, and spread them out 4 inches at a time. *Joanne Weber*

Jump No. 4 + Jump No. 3 + Jump No. 2 + Jump No. 1 + Finish + Target

This is just like the previous sequences. Make sure your helper is holding the dog far enough back from the fourth jump that she can get a good running start. The large dogs should be going fast enough to stretch the distance to ten feet between jumps by now. The slightly smaller dogs will need to gradually increase from 8 feet to 10, a half-foot at a time. Be very careful when you are setting your jumps. There should be exactly the same distance between the jumps.

If you are measuring from a certain point, such as the position of jump no. 4, which doesn't change, then remember that as you set your jump distances, you gain a foot for each jump you move toward the finish line. It is easiest to just put marks down on the floor or on your mats to avoid confusion. It is easy to get mixed up when doing this, especially if someone inexperienced is helping you. When you look at the floor, there should be an 8-foot mark (for jump no. 3) 8 feet from the no. 4 jump, and a 9-foot mark 1 foot away from that. Then, at jump no. 2, the 9-foot mark will be 2 feet away from the 8-foot mark, and at jump no. 1, the 9-foot mark will be 3 feet away from the 8-foot mark. Mats can stretch, so it is a much better idea to mark the actual surface of the floor. I use a paint pen to write on the cement floor in my training barn. If you do not own your facility, you can write on masking tape so that you know where to put your jumps.

The dog must now learn to turn 90 degrees and run back over the jumps. *Joanne Weber*

Your dog does not have to be doing single strides (singles) between jumps at 10 feet apart before moving on, but it helps. When the dog is doing well repeatedly, go on. As long as a dog is doing singles, it's okay for the jumps to be only 9 feet apart. Make sure you are giving the reward well past the finish line, as you want the dog to continue running fast way beyond the finish.

1/4 Turn + Jump No. 4 + Jump No. 3 + Jump No. 2 + Jump No. 1 + Finish + Target

Next, have the helper turn the dog slightly (about 90 degrees), so that your dog must *turn* and run to the no. 4 jump.

1/2 Turn + Jump No. 4 + Jump No. 3 + Jump No. 2 + Jump No. 1 + Finish + Target

Have the helper turn the dog all the way around (180 degrees) so that the dog must *turn around* and run to the no. 4 jump.

The dog makes a 180-degree turn to run over the jumps. *Joanne Weber*

Angle Off To The Side + Jump No. 4 + Jump No. 3 + Jump No. 2 + Jump No. 1 + Finish + Target

Have the helper hold the dog a little off to one side of the mat so that the dog has to aim for that no. 4 jump instead of cutting the corner and running straight toward the finish line. This is necessary in case the dog ever drops or fumbles the ball during play. The dog must go back to that no. 4 jump, no matter how far out of line he had to chase a rolling ball.

Leave the dog with the helper and walk around the far side of the jump. Touch the upright. Look at the dog. Pat the 8-inch board. Say, "Jump, Jump, Jump," or whatever you usually say when your dog is taking the series of jumps. Take a few steps toward the finish line so that you are between the no. 4 and no. 3 jumps, off to the far side of the racing lane. Get the dog psyched up and you take off running toward the finish line.

The helper lets go when you start running. The dog will beat you to the finish line, so *throw the target* well *past* the finish line, so it will be there first, that is, if your dog jumped as requested. Do angles off to the right and left, and *move* progressively *further out,* a little at a time, until the dog will run back to the no. 4 jump from 10 to 15 feet out of the lane.

Karli is practicing "angle jumping" to remind her that, no matter what, she must return to that no. 4 jump on her way back. This is done from both sides of the racing lane. *Joanne Weber*

NOTE: By now, the dog must either know the box (from practicing it separately), or you will have to have a helper bounce a ball for your dog near the box.

Box (Pedal + Catch + Turn & Run) + Jump No. 4 + Jump No. 3 + Jump No. 2 + Jump No. 1 + Finish + Target

Stand within 14 feet of the box. Have the helper encourage the dog to hit the box. Let go of the dog and turn and run beside the jumps toward the finish line. The dog should run to the box, hit it, catch the ball, turn and run back over the jumps. He should beat you to the finish area, so be ready to throw the target well past the finish. The moment the ball is in your dog's mouth, call him excitedly as you turn and run.

For dogs who do not know the box yet: The helper bounces the ball near the front of the box. If the dog accidentally runs into the box, or uses it as a turning board, all the better.

The box is added at this point. If the dog has not learned the box, he can just get a ball that your helper bounces for him. The dog must get the ball, turn and run over all four jumps to the finish, where his target will be waiting. *Joanne Weber*

Jump + Box (Or Ball) + Jump No. 4 + Jump No. 3 + Jump No. 2 + Jump No. 1 + Finish + Target

Start between jumps no. 4 and no. 3. Let the dog run to the box over jump no. 4 and run back over all of the jumps to the finish. The following three steps are very important. Do not skip ahead because you know by now that your dog will do this. Back up *one jump at a time*, and do each one until your dog is doing it well.

The dog is held in front of jump no. 4. He should jump, hit the box, and complete the chain of all four jumps. If the owner can't run fast enough to beat the dog to the finish line, he will have to throw the target into the run-back area so that it will be there for the dog when he finishes. Or a helper could release the dog at the no. 4 jump while the owner waits at the finish line. *Joanne Weber*

Jump No. 3 + Jump No. 4 + Box + Jump No. 4 + Jump No. 3 + Jump No. 2 + Jump No. 1 + Finish + Target

Back up to between jumps no. 3 and no. 2. Do the same as before. The dog will be jumping no. 3 and no. 4, hitting the box, turning and running back over jumps no. 4, no. 3, no. 2 and no. 1.

Jump No. 2 + Jump No. 3 + Jump No. 4 + Box + Jump No. 4 + Jump No 3 + Jump No. 2 + Jump No. 1 + Finish + Target

Back up to between jumps no. 2 and no. 1 and do it again. Keep chaining—you're almost there!

The dog is held in front of jump no. 3. The owner can run back toward the finish line after releasing the dog, or a helper can release the dog and step out of the way so that the owner can call the dog back to the finish line. *Joanne Weber*

The dog is held in front of jump no. 2. It is very important not to skip steps. This is the point where many people want to skip ahead too fast. They end up with a dog who, when released at the start line, will jump two jumps and stop. *Joanne Weber*

Jump No. 1–Jump No. 4 + Box + Jump No. 4–Jump No. 1 + Finish + Target

Back up to the starting line to release the dog over all four jumps.

Congratulations. If you've gotten this far, your dog has learned the basics of Flyball training. However, you're not done yet.

The dog is now being held in front of jump no. 1 and doing the complete behavior chain. *Joanne Weber*

Your dog has learned the main Flyball sequence, but is not the only dog on the team. Now you have to start backing up, 3 to 5 feet at a time, and keep practicing until the dog will run at the jumps from 25 to 30 feet back from the starting line.

The dog now knows his job, and races across the start to complete the chain of behaviors he has learned. His target object will be waiting for him at the finish, for his reward. *Joanne Weber*

Most mid-sized dogs can reach top speed in about three strides, or about 20 feet. This means we want to let them go at least this far from the starting line to achieve maximum speed during the individual dog's run.

Lie Down is a command all Flyball dogs should respond to instantly. It means to drop immediately and remain in place until told to move. It's much easier for me to control my dogs by placing them on a command and putting them on their "honor."

Chapter 6

Additional Training

Control Exercises

For optimum safety in playing Flyball, your dog should have a few basic control exercises down pat. I think that what amazes spectators most at Flyball tournaments is how dogs can practice such remarkable control amid all the excitement. Some of the dogs have never had any formal obedience training, but they have learned some Flyball "survival skills." Following are some commands that are important to work on if you plan to get your dog into Flyball competition.

Come When Called

It is obvious that if you do not have a dog who will come when called, then you need to do some training. If the dog is not reliable with coming back to you, you will not be able to safely practice off-leash, and much of the Flyball training takes place off-leash. In addition, if you practice outdoors in the summer, a dog that cannot be trusted off-leash might run into the road or run after the neighbor's dogs or horses and get seriously injured. Please make sure your dog will come when called if you want to progress with training.

Teaching the Come When Called

The Come command for Flyball is different from one you would teach for an Obedience ring. You do not use the dog's name, followed by the command, Come, as you would in Obedience. In Flyball, every second counts, and we teach the dog to spin around and come immediately when the name is yelled in an enthusiastic manner.

One member of my team first started coming to practice and her dog was very excited and wanted to run all over the place, chasing other dogs. I said that her dog needed some work on the Recall, and pretty soon I noticed her in another part of the training building, leaving the dog on a Sit-Stay, going to the end of the leash and saying, "Willie, come!" She could have done this all night, and it probably wouldn't teach the dog to come, especially when chasing after other dogs. I quickly demonstrated what I had in mind, and made a mental note that I should never assume that what I'm thinking and what people are hearing are the same thing!

To teach the kind of Recall that will stop a highly excited dog on a dime, you have to practice this as an exercise. You can use a long line or a retractable leash. Wait until the dog has become engrossed in something exciting. At this point, you call the dog's name sharply and excitedly, and run backwards, letting the dog chase you as you go. After the name (about one-half second after), you will apply a firm jerk to the leash as you run away from the dog. The dog is learning that he must respond quickly to these random Recalls. Lots of praise and the dog's target await him if he is quick to respond to your call.

Lie Down

Sometimes it is important to stop a dog immediately, or "park" him quickly while you take care of something. The emergency Down command works well for this. Make sure that your dog understands that when he hears this command, he is to drop in his tracks and not move until told to do so. This also sometimes helps when trying to catch a "runaway" dog.

Teaching the Lie Down

Again, I use a completely different method for teaching what I call the "emergency Down," meaning drop immediately from anywhere, than I would to teach the Down at Heel position in one of my obedience classes. Start out with the dog in a Sit position, facing you. Get the dog's attention focused on a very juicy treat in your left hand. Hold your right arm and hand up with the palm open. Your left hand will be dashing to the floor with the treat an instant *before* the right hand makes the signal. Both of your arms will be suddenly opening in opposite directions, like the jaws of an alligator. I also sometimes refer to this as the "alligator Down."

The trick is to get your left hand, the one with the treat, into motion slightly ahead of your right hand. If focused on the right hand, your dog will then just glance up at it when you thrust open your arms. You want the dog's nose firmly "attached" to the treat in your left hand, so that when you quickly bring it down, the dog will flatten on the ground to follow the goodie.

The dog may not even be seeing the signal at this point. That's okay. With luck, your dog is catching it in his peripheral vision, and may even try to "duck" because of something suddenly shooting up toward the ceiling. That's okay, it may actually help the dog drop faster. However, you don't ever want your dog to think this is a threatening gesture, and at no time will you ever use your right hand to give a Down correction.

The dog will go down quickly just for food. The raised Down signal will become the cue for a fast drop. When the dog is performing reliably directly in front of you, you can begin having your dog drop while you are moving. While walking with the dog on your left, have your food in the left hand, and give the signal with your right again as you squat forward with your body (don't turn and face the dog to do this).

Whether or not you use a verbal command Down in the initial training steps of this exercise depends on whether your dog already knows what Down means. If your dog already has learned another form of Down on command, you can use that Down command as you sweep the food toward the floor and give the signal. If this is a new exercise for your dog, you will want to get the behavior established first, and then name it ("Lie Down") for your dog. If your dog is sluggish responding to the Down command, you may want to start over with a different command word to try to eliminate the sluggish response for this exercise.

As the dog learns to drop instantly while moving, you can start the drop at different times and locations. While training, if the dog goes down quickly upon request, you should always give something wonderful like a treat, a ball, a play session or other instant reinforcement as a reward. Later, when the behavior is under stimulus control, you will not have to immediately reward or release when your dog complies. Remember to use a variable schedule of reward to wean your dog off the idea of getting something every time. This will also strengthen the response to any command.

Leave It!

Leave It means, "Do not touch it!" Flyball is a very exciting, fast-paced sport. The dogs become very anxious to join in the chasing and fun. Dogs that are the best at Flyball are also the ones who love to chase things like livestock, rodents, or other dogs, so don't be discouraged if your dog wants to go after the other dogs. This is natural. However, this is also unacceptable, and you must immediately discourage your dog from doing it.

No aggression is tolerated in the sport of Flyball, and a dog can be banned for life for attacking another dog in competition.

Teaching the Leave It

The best way to teach this is to set up your dog to want to chase or "go for" another dog, then give a sound correction while shouting, "Leave it!" You absolutely must convince the dog that chasing other dogs is hazardous to his health. This is serious business. Shaking your finger and saying "no, no, Fluffy" is not going to work. A good place to position your dog for this is right next to the finish line. How hard a reprimand you give depends on how seriously you want your dog to take this. A serious offense calls for a serious solution.

Stay

Staying put is a good thing for a dog to be able to do. We expect our dogs to Stay when we give the Lie Down command. We do not want such good control, however, that you could leave your dog on a Sit-Stay at the end of the jumps and walk to the other end and call her over the jumps. Flexibility is important. If your dog is too controllable at Flyball practice, then she doesn't want to play Flyball badly enough!

Teaching the Stay

The only thing different about a Flyball Stay is that it is performed around many distractions and amid total chaos.

You can teach this exercise just as you would for obedience class: having the dog stay and not letting him make a mistake by remaining close to him and praising for success at close range (heel position, then one arm's length). When the dog has the concept of staying where he was told "down," then you can begin adding the distractions until you can eventually trust the dog to stay at Flyball practice or a tournament. The correction for getting up is to place the dog back into the Down (or Sit) position.

There should not be any scary corrections or yells of, "No!" You simply return, gently (without saying a word), put the dog back in the exact position as when you left and continue with what you were doing. Praise the dog with "good Stay" to show your dog that is what you wanted.

Dogs seem to learn quickly that if they are patient and do what they are told, they will eventually get their turn to play Flyball. It amazes spectators sometimes to see dogs in such control when they want to play so badly. I guess they realize that it is futile to try to get up and help themselves to a turn, so they might as well wait until it's really time.

Out

If your dog does not give up the ball when he brings it back, you need to get a command which means drop it. In a competition, you may get flagged and have to turn around and rerun your dog. That would be a little hard with a ball already in his mouth. Tugging and playing keep-away is okay, but a dog should give it up on command.

Teaching the Out

To teach giving the ball up on command, you can start by offering something in exchange. This could be a treat, a toy or another ball. The dog reluctant to give up the ball doesn't want to lose the prize. Remember, the best prize is always given at the end, and a dog should be very willing to give up a ball for the target. Place your hand on the ball in the dog's mouth and say, "out" as you produce another ball (or treat) for your dog to take. Don't pull on the ball. This encourages the dog to hold on tighter! If you want the dog to drop the ball, try gently pushing it back further into the throat. When your dog's mouth opens, say, "good Out."

Building Vocabulary

There are a few basic words, not necessarily commands, that your dog should learn. Here are a few of them with their meanings. Dogs may or may not come to know the meaning of these words, but there's no harm in using them and trying to build your dog's understanding of what's going on.

READY? This word is meant to excite. It means that the dog is about to race. Your dog could also take it to mean, "line up and get ready."

SET! This can be used as in, "ready . . . set . . . go." Set is when we release the dogs (it means "go!"). They never actually hear the word, "go" as they should be crossing the starting line, 20 feet away from you, by that time.

GET YOUR BALL! Use this to "pump up" your dog before a race, or use it to send a dog back for a dropped ball. It is meant to get the dog to focus on the box end.

DOG'S NAME! This should produce an instant Recall with a flip turn off the box and a burst of speed. It should also produce an instant Recall any time you want your dog to come back to you. Dogs should not take off down to the box without being sent.

FALSE START   Say this to calm your dog down when the first dog has false started in a race. It means, "I'm sorry, but you're not going to run this time. It's beyond my control. You're still a good dog, and you will get to play eventually, but just not right now."

JUMP!   If your dog fumbles the ball and goes out of the line of jumps, this can get the dog to angle back in to the fourth jump. Some people use it at the box, to remind the dog of the next thing to do.

BIG JUMPS   Say this to your dog if your team has had to pull the smallest dog, and the jump heights have gone up. I don't know how much good it does, but it you say it often enough, the dog may come to understand that there are now higher jumps. This is important if you did not warm up at the taller height. You don't get a chance to practice over the higher jumps once you're racing.

QUIET!   While at a tournament, your dog will spend a good deal of time in a crate or waiting to race. It is a good idea for all dogs to know what it means to stop barking or whining.

HURRY UP   Before or between races, you will want to exercise your dogs. A word like "hurry" or "potty" is useful. You want the dog to get down to business quickly.

KENNEL   This just tells the dog to get into the crate.

STOP IT!   This is used to get the dog to stop doing anything—twisting in circles, nipping the person in front of you, clawing the mat, whatever.

Proofing Against Distractions

Once the basics of Flyball competition have been learned, your dog must be prepared for things that may happen in a real tournament, such as another dog passing both ahead of and after him. Dogs must be able to change lanes and not become confused and cross over to the other side. They must be able to run while another team is running in the other lane. They are going to have to do all of this amidst the deafening noise of dozens of dogs barking. In addition, we want to prepare and proof against unforeseen situations that may occur during racing or at a tournament.

Loose Balls

There are not supposed to be any loose balls lying around at a tournament, but sometimes one gets kicked out into the racing area, or another dog drops the ball during a run. To proof against this, practice with one or more loose balls lying about. Of course, you will have to make a correction if the dog goes for the "planted" ball. Interrupt if the dog starts to go for one of your "decoy" balls and remind your dog to focus on the ball at the box and on the target object.

Knocked-Down Jumps

Occasionally, a dog will knock down jumps or break boards on jumps. There is not always time during racing for someone to run out and correct the situation. So, it is best if the dog is just taught to jump over jumps that are lying on their sides. There will be no penalty for jumping such a jump in a tournament, provided the dog does not run around it.

The dog should get used to jumping over a knocked-down jump in practice in case it happens at a tournament. *Joanne Weber*

Stray Dogs (Interference)

Every now and then, the opposing team has a new dog who is not "lane sure." This dog may run over to your lane or chase your dog. You can prepare for this situation by turning loose a confused dog at practice.

Praise your dog for still jumping the jumps and bringing the ball, even though another dog was trying to block the path or boggle her up.

Flags

Some Line Judges get carried away with their flag waving, and it may pose a distraction if your dog is bothered by that sort of thing. You can proof train this by having someone sit there in practice and wave flags.

Run-Back Area

You could encounter just about anything in the run-back area. People are there waving Frisbees® or balls around, wrestling with their dogs, feeding them treats and all sorts of things. If your dog is easily distracted by these things, or by the presence of the other team's returning dogs barreling down the runway just a few feet from your lane, work on the Leave It command and set your dog up with practice so that you can correct this.

Training Problems

If you have used the backward chaining method described in this book and followed the training sequences properly, your dog should not develop any of the problems listed in this chapter. If you are training a new dog and start to experience any of these problems, go back to the behavior chain and start over. Be careful not to progress until the dog understands the current sequence you are training.

If you have a previously trained dog who has learned with some other method you may find some of the solutions in this chapter helpful. However, you always have the option of going back to the behavior chaining and starting all over, even if you feel the dog is fully trained. I observe many dogs with a lack enthusiasm for the sport. They should have never gotten past the first link of the behavior chaining sequence—restrained Recalls past the finish line. If the dog cannot be motivated enough to get really excited about whatever you are using for a target, you are not going to have much success with the subsequent steps of Flyball training.

Box Problems

Hesitation at the Box

If you have done much of your training without an assistant, you may have at some time left the dog on a Stay and gone behind the box yourself to load and give encouragement to the dog. Although this saves a lot of walking back and forth, you should be aware that you could be teaching the dog that reinforcement comes from the person at the box. I had trained a Golden Retriever this way, and every time she caught the ball from the box, she looked to the loader as if to say, "See what a good girl I am?" She would sometimes delay her return by several seconds, waiting for the box loader to praise her for a job well done. She would be oblivious to my frantic calls and praise. If this dog missed the ball, she would go after it and come straight back without a problem, but when she caught it, she was expecting some kind of commendation from the person at the box.

The dog may be hesitating at the box to chew the ball before starting back. This can be remedied with the use of a retractable long line. As you and the dog run toward the box, and as the dog hits the pedal, press the button on the retractable leash and give a jerk backward as soon as your dog has the ball.

Proper timing is critical. If you jerk too soon or too late, you might confuse the dog. After the correction, give lots of excited praise as you let go of the button on the leash and run back toward the starting line with his target object. You can also practice a Get It and Go away from the box if you don't want to give your dog a correction at the box.

Teaching the Swimmer's Turn
One way of getting a more efficient turn at the box is by using a highway cone to teach the flow pattern of the turn. By centering the cone 2 to 3 feet in front of the box, the dog will have to head slightly to the left to get around the cone. He will hit the box, then come off the box, turning to his right and coming around the other side of the cone. This type of traffic flow encourages a "U-turn," resembling a swimmer's turn. This enables the dog to get up onto the box with all four of his legs, which helps absorb the shock and allows the dog to kick off with his powerful back legs.

First, you must know which way your dog turns off the box. If he comes off to the right, then you should have the cone slightly off center to the right. If he turns off to the left, move the cone slightly to the left, as he will be aproaching the box from the right side of the cone. The purpose of moving the cone right or left is so as not to impede the dog's forward momentum in approaching the box. In other words, you do not want him screeching to a halt, veering out and making a circle around the cone.

Training for this must begin on leash, to guide the dog through the traffic pattern. Start by taking it slow and then allow your dog to increase his approach speed. Eventually you can work the dog off leash. Some dogs will still want to hit and push off with only their front feet. If you want to ensure that your dog pushes off with his back legs each time, I would suggest you use this method in combination with shaping with a clicker, and reward the dog each time he shoves off correctly with his back legs.

Hitting the Top of the Box

If you have taught your dog that the box involves a pedal press rather than a "swimmer's turn," you may find the dog trying to make contact with the top of the box rather than the pedal. This is only possible, of course, with boxes that have a top (a horizontal surface of some kind above the pedal). Wedge-shaped boxes or full-faced pedals do not encourage the dog to make this type of error.

The dog could be hitting the box somewhere other than the pedal for various reasons.

First, there is a possibility that at some point the dog has pinched a pad between the pedal and the vertical surface of the box. If you suspect that this has happened, do not be too demanding. Back up and encourage the dog to begin hitting the pedal again. Do not reward any attempts to hit the box anywhere other than the pedal.

Another reason that the dog may stop hitting the pedal is because the behavior has been extinguished. Where do you keep your Flyball box during the day while you are gone? A dog with access to it may have just spent the day pressing the pedal trying to get a ball and not receiving any, thereby learning that pressing the pedal doesn't produce balls. Go back to the steps teaching the pedal push, and keep the box out of the dog's reach when you are not there. It could also help if you put something on top of the box to prevent the dog from trying to press there. Make it look less like a pedal by placing an object (like a large toy truck) there.

Stealing the Ball from the Cup

Let's examine why you might be having this problem. Again, if you have taught your dog that the Flyball box is a banking surface, rather than a pedal to be pressed, you should not be having this problem. In addition, many of the boxes in use at this time have the ball in a cup which is built into the front of the box, rather than being in an exposed throwing arm. The enclosed cups have made it quite difficult for a dog to get the ball out without triggering the box, especially if the cup is part of the pedal. The older boxes with the exposed throwing arm would make it possible for the dog to try to take the ball directly from the cup. There are also new boxes in use which use no cup at all and the ball just sits on top of the box to be batted into the air by a moving bar.

The best way to prevent ball stealing is to go back and teach that the box is a turning surface that conveniently spits out a tennis ball while the dog is banking off of it. If you have one of the older style boxes, which has the more horizontal pedal and the exposed throwing arm, this would be difficult to do. Here are some alternate suggestions:

1. Always cover the cup with your hand or foot if the dog tries to go straight for the ball.

2. If your throwing arm is behind the box, prevent the dog from getting around the box by placing some form of barricade (chairs or milk crates will work) on either side of the box.

3. Build a chute up to the box with some form of fencing, which would give your dog access only to the front of the box.

If you are using one of the new boxes with no cup at all, you should use a different box to train the new dogs. Our team uses this type of box, but when we introduce the training sequences to a beginner dog, we use a full-face pedal, 45-degree-angle box. Only after the dog has the complete behavior chain mastered and knows what the box is for (turning) do we load a ball in this "cupless" box.

If you have one of the boxes with the cup in the vertical face or pedal, the dog might not be able to get the ball out with his mouth, but you may have a dog who tries to paw the ball out of the box. If this is happening, you have moved ahead too fast in your training. The box should be used as a turning surface, and if the dog does not hit the pedal (by either method outlined in this book), you have no business loading the cup yet. If you do, you will be changing the focus from hitting the pedal to diving after a ball.

Wide Turns off the Box

The dog should virtually ricochet off the box pedal, whipping around to come back over the jumps. Dogs that come off the box making a wide turn to the right or left are usually not in a hurry. Examine your training sequences and see if you chained the behaviors properly. Before this habit becomes ingrained in a dog, try to correct it with behavior chaining (no part of the chain involves making a wide arc to turn around). If you used some other method to train and want a few ideas to cure your dog's bad habit, here are some things you can try:

- Use a turning board to prevent the dog from turning out. A turning board is just a piece of plywood measuring about two feet square, which the loader will place to the side of the box in the direction the dog usually turns. Later, you can diminish the size of this physical barrier so it acts as a reminder to keep the turns tight.

- The loader can bend down and use her body as a block alongside the box as a reminder to the dog. Of course, you could try to correct this problem with a well-timed correction on a retractable lead also. I feel it is better to have the dog learn to turn himself, rather than be jerked through the air.

Ball Problems

Ball problems come in a variety of forms. Some dogs chew on the ball as if it were a big wad of bubble gum. Other dogs drop the ball prematurely, before they cross the finish line. There are ball-shy dogs who don't try to catch the ball at all, and there are dogs who are so ball-crazy that they will forget what they are doing and go for any stray ball in sight.

While there is no rule against chewing the ball, you would be better off to have the dog hold the ball firmly with no chewing. Ball-chewing dogs can accidentally lose their grasp on the ball, often letting it fall from their mouths on the way back. Additionally, the dog cannot be giving full concentration and energy to running while wasting brain cells and energy gnawing on the ball all the way back. To help prevent this problem, use firm, new tennis balls, which are not so chewy. In addition, work on the Hold It command. You can also make a dog covet the ball more if you play tug-of-war games with the ball. This encourages the dog to clamp down on the ball and not release it.

If your dog is dropping the ball at the finish line in anticipation of receiving a treat, work on the Hold It command, letting the dog spit the ball only into your hand and never onto the floor. Teach the dog that a dropped ball must be picked up again and handed to you before getting the treat. If you are using a motivational target, just don't give the reward unless your dog brings the ball all the way back.

These activities teach the dog that the way to win the reward or target object is to hang onto the ball until you invite him to exchange it for the target. You may have to hide the target from view until your dog has come all the way back. He still knows you have it, and is running back for the target, but with some dogs, seeing it is just too much excitement.

Remember, the reward for completing the behavior chain correctly is getting the target. This includes coming well past the finish line with the ball.

A ball-shy dog may be hesitant to catch the ball. Perhaps the dog has been hit in the nose by a tennis ball at some point, or has had a sore tooth or a gum problem. Whatever the reason, this dog has to learn that the ball will not hurt, especially if he catches it properly instead of letting it hit him in the face. If you have checked out any possible medical problems, go back to the section on teaching the dog to catch. Start over by using something soft and harmless, like a sponge ball or a rolled up pair of socks. When you have your dog catching this reliably, switch back to the standard tennis ball (or whatever size regulation ball you would normally use).

If your dog misses the ball and does not make an attempt to go after it, you have possibly pushed ahead too fast, stressing speed before the dog understood all the separate parts of the game. If you have been in the habit of using a retractable leash and jerking at the instant the dog catches the ball, you may have made the dog think that running back quickly is more important than bringing the ball. You may have jerked the leash too soon, before the dog's mouth was around the ball, correcting the dog for trying to catch it. If this is the case, you will have to back up and go through the steps again, showing that you do want the dog to take the time to run after those missed balls. Use lots of encouragement.

If you have a dog that is not really ball-crazy, or only likes moving or airborne balls, you will need to reinforce your retrieve training. Insist that the dog returns with the ball.

Everyone's favorite dog to train for Flyball is the "tennis ball junkie." This type of dog loves the ball and would do anything to get one (or more). This trait can prove to be a problem, however. This dog wants any and all balls. If a ball rolls out onto the course during a run, he may leave the racing lane and run after the stray ball. This dog might even try to evade the owner at the finish line, run back over the jumps and try to get another ball—even with one in his mouth already!

You can "proof" the dog by setting loose balls out on the course and correcting him for going after them. You can do your best to safeguard against any loose balls lying around on the floor at a tournament. Tell the box loader to wait a safe amount of time before reloading after this dog is on the way back to the finish line. If the ball is loaded too quickly, the dog may hear the box being cocked and become so excited thinking about getting an additional ball so as to turn right around and run back down to the box again. This dog needs to be convinced that the target is at the finish line, *not* at the box. The ball (or other target) at the finish should always be what the dog is working towards.

"Montana," a Golden Retriever owned by Patty Merritt of Warren, Michigan, is truly a ball glutton. He got three balls into his mouth and was still trying to pick up a fourth one!

Jump Problems

A common jumping problem is when a dog skirts around one or more of the jumps. The dog is most likely to do this on the jump closest to the box in the event the ball is missed and bounces too far out of alignment with the racing lane. The dog will also sometimes skirt the last jump when coming across the finish line if the handler moves out to the side to allow room for the next dog to be sent. Most jumping problems of this nature can be avoided if the dog is properly introduced to the jumping exercise with behavior chaining, and understands that the requirement is for the dog to jump all four jumps, both ways, no matter what.

The way to proof the dog to come over the jump at the box end (the no. 4 jump) is to deliberately send the ball out of alignment with the jumps. Position the box, or just a placed ball, 15 to 20 feet beyond the last jump, but place it slightly off the centerline of the jumps to the right or left. As you continue to move it out little by little, there may be a point where the dog decides it would be shorter to just cut back to the no. 3 jump, skipping the fourth one. This is where you will have to run down to the end, so that when your dog turns around with the ball, you will be there at the no. 4 jump, encouraging and coaxing the dog over. Practice moving the box (or ball) over in both directions from the course.

Most of the time, a dog who understands the jumping sequence will not skirt the no. 1 jump just because the handler has stepped off to the side a little. But if a dog does this, a review of the jump training sequences is necessary.

It is more likely that the dog is fearful or has had a bad experience with the dog coming toward him. This is actually more of a passing problem, and it involves teaching the dog that the oncoming dog is not going to plow into him, bite him, steal the ball or otherwise bother him. You should proof this until the dog is steady enough to fly through the jump at the same time the other dog is flying through from the opposite direction (provided both dogs' bodies will fit simultaneously between the 24-inch jumps). See the section on passing for instructions.

If you have had the problem of the dog knocking down the jumps or charging down the course breaking boards without even blinking, your dog has great drive! But, she needs to learn a little "lift." Practice jumping the dog at a height which is 1 to 2 inches higher than it would normally be in competition, so that she will put a little more oomph into the leap. Some teams pad the top board with foam pipe insulation material. While this may prevent the dog from injury when hitting a jump, it does not teach the dog not to slam into it in the first place.

There have been several proposals to change the rules to allow a foam top board or other devices to remedy the problem of dogs hitting the top board and breaking it. This does not address the fact that these dogs have not been properly trained to clear the jump. At our tournaments, we always make sure we have lots of extra boards on hand, especially the 1-inch boards, which can break quite easily. If you have a dog who cannot run in competition without repeatedly shattering the jumps, that dog probably should not be exhibited. It looks bad to the spectators. Either teach your dog to jump, get a short dog on the team to lower the jump height or stop racing that dog.

Aggression Problems

Many dogs have very powerful chase instincts, and it is difficult for them to maintain self-control during the excitement of Flyball competition. Some dogs just chase other dogs for fun, others are jealous of the other dog's ball and still others have malicious intent on their minds. As previously mentioned, whatever the reason, Flyball dogs must be cured of going after other dogs.

One way to do this is to teach the dog the Leave It command. This involves the use of a strong negative reinforcer whenever the dog is aggressing toward another dog. When the dog has a basic grasp of the concept of Leave It (which means, "Back off now!"), test this by placing him right at the starting line and make the dog be a perfect angel. The dog must learn that there's just no good outcome in trying to run after the other dogs. Another thing to consider is that if your dog is watching or running after other dogs, he is not very well focused on the business at hand. Make sure your dog's target is the only focus during racing.

Passing Problems

Dogs should be cured of any aggression problems before beginning passing. Passing should be introduced gradually, with the returning dogs passing stationary ones. The first real passes should take place many feet back from the actual starting line (see the portion of this section on teaching passing).

Dogs that stop or slow down at the finish line have not been trained to come back to a target. Dogs should think that the finish is actually about 20 feet past the actual line. Encourage the dogs to keep running at top speed well past the finish. In practice, the target should be thrown well past the run-back area so that the dogs do not slow down to stop right after finishing. If the dog is stopping or turning at the finish in order to chase the next dog, then see the section on aggression in this chapter.

If a dog tries to run away after finishing, use an emergency Down command. A dog who freezes before the last jump (or anywhere else on the course) is a dog that does not want to have a ball taken away. Proper use of a target object would help this dog to relax about what he has. Your dog should believe that there will be something even better *after* the finish. If your dog does not use a target, avoid just taking the ball away or snapping on the leash right after he returns. Spend a few seconds playing tug-of-war with the ball before you make the dog give it up.

A dog that has had a bad experience or collision with another dog at the finish line will try to avoid it and may even refuse the closest jump.

The snow fence lines the jumps to help dogs learn the jumping sequence without making mistakes.

The best you can do is to slowly rebuild confidence by showing that nothing is going to hurt the dog at the finish line. This may take time. While you are working on it, you may have to run the dog last on the team to avoid the problem.

If you practice indoors, with one mat down for the racing lane, the dogs will be less likely to run around the jump, because they feel safer on the rubber mat. If you practice outdoors, it is just as easy for the dog to run out around the jumps if they feel the least bit threatened by the oncoming dog.

To help the dogs learn confidence in passing, use the chutes (made of the 2-foot-high snow fence). We have fence stakes that push into the ground and hold up the snow fence ($1.49 each at any farm store). These are plastic poles with a metal stake in the bottom, meant for use in stringing electric fence wire. The snow fence hooks easily onto these posts. We extend the chute well beyond the finish line on both sides, which forces the dogs to pass each other without going out around the jumps. We begin by doing "safety passing" and gradually have the dogs pass closer and closer to the start/finish line.

Keenan: A Case Study

Keenan is a Belgian Tervuren who has been running Flyball for several years. He is capable of running it in under 4.9 seconds. However, after a serious crash at one tournament when a dog was released too soon, his confidence was shattered and he developed some neurotic behavior. The crash took place as Keenan was returning over the jumps, and it caused

The 2" boards on the ground are to help the dog with his take-off and landing point. The boards are there to keep the dog from starting or ending his leap too close to the jump.

him to smash into the jump. After the crash, he would still run well down to the box, but on the way back, he would often miss one or more jumps. Sometimes it was all of the jumps, but it was usually the jumps closest to the finish line.

During a seminar I gave for Keenan's team, we examined the problem. It seemed to be a case of "location avoidance." Keenan had great form going, but slowed down and "stutter-stepped" on the way back. We tried placing smaller boards before and after the Flyball jumps to help him space his jumping strides better. This helped a little.

I had Keenan's owner, Debbie, practice some restrained Recalls. Then I asked her and the loader, Dave, to switch places. With Debbie at the box end and Keenan running to Dave, the dog's form was perfect, without hesitation.

Then I had Debbie step behind the box and load for Keenan, with Dave sending him. Keenan stutter-stepped slowly to the box, and raced back to Dave with perfect form. This was just the opposite of what he was doing before. He had somehow associated running toward Debbie with his jumping mishap.

Keenan, a Belgian Tervuren owned by Dave and Debbie McFarlane, developed a jumping phobia after colliding with another dog and smashing into the jumps. He was taking off too soon, jumping too high, and landing just on the other side of the hurdle.

We gradually got Keenan used to performing in both directions correctly by having Debbie run alongside the jumps with him and having Dave send him until the dog did it correctly enough times and forgot which location he was trying to avoid in the first place. Now he is back to his old self, running under five seconds.

A handler's-eye view of the previous handler calling her dog back. It's important to keep your body out of the way so that the person behind you can judge the release point accurately. *Joanne Weber*

Chapter 7

Teamwork

Passing

Passing is a skill every member of the Flyball team must learn. Your team-mates do not want to lose a race by the width of *your* late pass. The team also does not want to lose the race because of a flagged (penalized) pass. To become skilled at passing, you have to work out a precise timing point and take-off point for each dog you will be running, and for each dog your dog(s) will be passing. As soon as your dog understands Flyball from the start to the finish line, you can begin mastering the most important part of the sport—passing.

Traffic Flow Pattern

When in practice or at a tournament, the handlers "load up" from the right, and call the dogs back to the left. The dogs need to learn this pattern so that they will not create traffic hazards, plowing into other dogs and tripping up handlers. Get the departing dogs used to being lined up off the mat on the right side (as you look down to the box end). When it is their turn to run, step onto the mat and position yourself at your start-ing mark. Place your dog's front feet even with the mark. When you re-lease your dog, you can run up closer to the start, if you like, to shout encouragement to the dog. Stay to the left of the mat and face toward your lane so that you are aware of the other traffic. Keep your body out of the way of the next handler, or he will not see his timing point to know when to release his dog. You can bend over into the lane or hold your target hand out into the middle so that your dog sees this as he returns back through the jump uprights. Make sure you do not interfere with or distract the dog that has to follow yours. Run back and off toward the left side of your racing lane so that the departing dog will have the center of the mat to himself. Collect your dog in the run-back area and move clear of the other returning dogs to avoid being bowled over. Keep this in mind as you start teaching your dog the following steps.

Standing Still

Get the dog used to passing by holding him still, somewhere between the 15- and 20-foot lines, as measured back from the starting line. Let a seasoned dog run the course and return. Do not release your dog, but watch his reaction. If he tries to get after the returning dog, correct him, and keep him focused down toward the Flyball box. Have the dogs take turns being the returning dog with another dog being held around the 15- to 20-foot lines.

Standing still passing involves not letting the second dog go at all. He just gets used to having another dog buzz past him. *Joanne Weber*

Moving On Leash

Using two dogs (both on leash), have one come over the first jump and finish line while the other goes toward the line and first jump. They should pass well back from the finish line. Make several more passes, each time having the dogs meet closer and closer to the first jump. You might have them both jumping the jump simultaneously from different directions, just to let them know they can. If either dog goes for the other dog, its owner must give it an immediate leash correction, accompanied with the Leave It command.

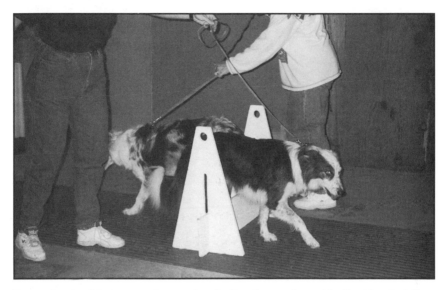

By moving beside one another on leash, the dogs get used to the idea that they can do it without crashing. They are learning the traffic flow pattern of "keep to the right." *Joanne Weber*

Safety Passing

With "safety passing," you are attempting what we would call a really bad pass (lots of room between the departing and returning dog). Your goal is to let go of your dog at the 20-foot line about the time the returning dog is almost past you. Run with him for a step or two, leaving your hand in the collar just in case he wants to snap at the other dog. Do the same thing as you gradually start letting him go as the returning dog is at 15, 12, 9, 6 and 3 feet. **Note:** all distances are measured from the starting line.

Precision Passing

To pass with any kind of precision, you must have less than 3 feet between your dog's nose and the finishing dog's nose. When you and your dog get

Safety passing involves letting the dogs go past each other way back from the start/finish line. *Joanne Weber*

this perfected, you will be working with pass evaluators, who will give you feedback on the accuracy of your pass. To have your dog's nose at the starting line at the precise instant the returning dog's nose crosses the finish line means that you will have to let go of your dog when the returning dog is still way out in the middle of the course. We have trained the dogs to be reliable, and they should not slow down at the finish line if they have been trained correctly, so you have nothing to worry about. Pass a dog who is similar in speed to your own dog. Stand at the 20-foot mark. Anticipate the returning dog's middle pounce (when his feet land between the third and second jumps on the way back). Release your dog at the same instant the returning dog's feet hit the mat. The returning dog has about 20 more feet to come. He is already at top speed, but he is expending slightly more effort because he has to clear the jumps. Your dog has to go "from 0 to 30 in 1 second." However, even though he is starting from a standstill, he is on the flat, so he can build up speed quickly.

Both dogs should reach the line at approximately the same time. If you are early (OOPS!) you will be flagged and have to rerun your dog at the end. If you are late, the time it takes your dog to reach the starting line after the other dog's nose finishes will be added to your dog's racing time. So you could have a really fast dog, but a lousy pass could add time to his

The release of these two dogs was timed for precision passing. Their two noses should touch the start/finish line marker at almost the same instant.

run. If I could equate time to distance, a fast dog can cover at least 20 feet per second. If your pass is late by 2 feet, that equates to one tenth of a second (.1). If your pass is 5 feet late (heaven forbid!), you have added a quarter-second to your dog's total time (not to mention your team's total time).

Since the dogs are placed on various teams according to their individual times under real racing conditions (including passes), it is in everyone's best interest to perfect their passes. A perfect pass is one in which an evaluator need only use the fingers of one hand to show the handler how close he is coming to a "nose to nose" pass (about 6 inches or less). An "okay" or "good" pass is one that is within one foot of being on the nose. Anything more than a foot off should be worked on, as it is slow.

Finding Your Take-Off Point

If the two dogs who are passing are running about the same speed, you should use the middle pounce as your *timing point* to release your dog. Your *take-off point* can be found by starting with your dog at the 19-foot or 20-foot line. If you are late or early on your pass, move up or back accordingly. For example, if you are letting your dog go at the 19-foot line and the pass evaluator is telling you that you are consistently 14 inches

This pass is too early. The departing dog crossed the start before the returning dog's nose hit the finish line. This would be flagged, and the early passing dog would have to be rerun after the fourth dog. *Joanne Weber*

This pass is just a little too late. The returning dog's nose has crossed the finish line, but the departing dog has not reached the start yet. This pass missed being perfect by about 1 foot. This will cost the team valuable tenths of seconds in a competition. *Joanne Weber*

This pass was close to perfect. Each dog's nose is now over the line by about 3 inches, which means if we could have gotten the picture one one-hundredth of a second sooner, their noses would both be touching the line. *Joanne Weber*

late, move forward to the 18-foot line to let your dog go. *Never change your timing point.* In other words, don't hesitate and wait longer for the returning dog to advance toward the start/ finish line. If you have to adjust your pass, monkey with your *where;* never change your *when.*

There are only two instances when you should vary from the "middle pounce" timing point. The first is if you have a little dog, an older dog, or a much slower dog than the one you are passing. If you let these dogs go at 20 feet, they will get tired quickly. Besides, the little dogs need a lot less room to get up to top speed. Ten to twelve feet is all they need. With the little dogs, I consistently use a different timing point. They are released when the returning dog is cresting the second jump. The same goes for slower dogs. Here is an example of how the math works. The returning dog is a 4.0-second dog. The passing dog is a 6.0-second dog. This is a ratio of 2:3. The returning dog, as he is cresting the second jump, has about 15 feet left to come. The passing dog has about 10 feet to go. The ratio is 3:2. The difference in speed is offset by the difference in distance, so that both dogs, ideally, will hit the start/ finish line at about the same time. Again, if you are early or late, work it out by moving forward or back with your take-off point, but don't try to adjust the point in time where the returning dog is coming back. It is just too hard to judge distances when you are looking at a moving object head on. That's why we need pass evaluators to tell us how our pass really looked.

For a little dog to pass a big dog, or a slower dog to pass a faster dog, the timing has to be carefully figured out. *Joanne Weber*

The only other time you should tamper with your timing point is when the returning dog's timing is off for some reason. If the dog ahead of yours fumbles the ball, stutter-steps, or in some other way changes his routine, you can expect that this dog will not be up to normal speed on the way back. If you see this happen, hold up on your pass just a fraction. Otherwise, you will probably be flagged for an early pass, and it will not be the dog's fault.

Using the Pass Evaluator

The pass evaluator will hold up his hands (or fingers) to give each handler an estimation of the distance by which his pass is too slow. If you have crossed before the returning dog finishes, you will be shown an "x," which indicates a flag or an early pass. A good evaluator will tell you by how much your pass was bad, so that you can make adjustments.

If you are consistently late by 2 feet at a certain line, you should move up 1 or 2 feet, but let go of the dog at the same point in time during the other dog's return (the middle bounce). If you are in a tournament and you get a flag and the evaluator is telling you that it was about 1 foot too early, then step back 1 foot from where you were, but let go of the dog at the same timing point as before.

At indoor tournaments, the take-off points are marked on tape that is put on the floor. At this outdoor (pole barn) tournament, the marks were spray painted on the sod, but this quickly wore off with all the traffic in the area, so my team put up the measurements on the wall of the barn and on the bleachers so that we could judge our take-off points. You can't have an accurate pass without knowing at what point you are releasing from.

Irregular Passing Situations

Sometimes you are forced to change positions on a team, or pass a different dog because of a substitution. If you have done your homework and practiced passing this dog, it should not be a problem. You may have one or two slow passes before you get your dog's confidence up after the initial change.

If the dog you are forced to pass has an inconsistent style, or tends to slow down after a few races, it becomes trickier. There is not much you can do when the returning dog slows down and makes you have a flagged pass. The best you can do is move up closer to the line and release your dog later (like on the bounce between second and first jumps). This will mean that your dog may not have time to be at top speed when he crosses the line, but it is better than getting a flagged pass each time. It would conserve team time and effort if the slow or inconsistent dog were put at the end, where no other dog would have to pass him.

Gut Instinct Passing

Gut instinct passing is what a lot of us relied upon years ago, before Flyball became so competitive. You could just kind of stand there at, oh, about that far from the starting line and let go of your dog when you felt it was right. This is not a reliable way of passing.

How can you make your pass tighter or slower if you don't know where and when you are releasing the dog in the first place? There are some people who are actually instinctively very good at this kind of passing. They could get their dog to pass anything from a cheetah to a sloth on the first try, getting it down to within a palm's width. These people are the exception, rather than the rule. It is very important to get your passes down straight. Only in the situation of irregular passing (as mentioned above) or some other unforeseen circumstance should anyone even remotely think they could rely on gut instinct.

Pass Evaluating

As a member of the team, all people must learn to pass evaluate. Your teammates are depending on your skill in estimating the correctness of their passes. Don't try to be nice. Try to be honest.

When any part of the returning dog's body comes over the finish line, take a mental photograph of what you see. How far back from that line was the departing dog? Make a determination, turn so the handler can see clearly, and hold up your hands or fingers to show a measurement of daylight between the two dogs' noses. If you thought the pass was absolutely perfect, nose to nose, no daylight, a real "gasper," almost a flag, "whew!" then show this by putting your two hands together (no daylight) or your thumb and first finger together, so that the handler knows this pass was perfect.

Try not to give signals like "thumbs-up" to mean a good pass. How good is "good?" The handler wants to know if there were inches or milli-meters to spare. The same goes for when a pass is early. We will all know when a pass is early at a tournament, as we will receive a flag. What the handler needs to know is *by how much*? Try to let the handler know if the pass was "really bad" or just off by a nose so that the person will know how to adjust the next pass.

The pass evaluator is the most important member of the team. Without feedback from someone standing at the start/finish line, you can only guess how good or bad your pass was. Races can be won or lost by the space of a bad pass.

The Starting Dog

The handler of the first dog on the team does not have to judge a pass, but must be very proficient at judging the start. When the Electronic Judging System is used, the handler must have the starts down to a science. The starting light sequence consists of a *blue* "stand-by" light, followed by two *amber* lights, then the *green* starting light. The amber and green lights are spaced in 1-second time intervals. The starting dog should be released on the second amber light at whatever distance he can travel in 1 second. This might be 16 feet or it might be 22 feet. Handlers must work out the timing for each dog's start. Some people prefer to let go of their dogs on the first amber light. Therefore, they release their dogs much further back (like at the 36-foot line). My feeling is that the dogs are running much more than necessary this way and there is a much greater chance for error the farther back your dog is released.

In situations where the Electronic Judging System is not used, the Head Judge will start the race with, "On your mark, get set, go." The judges are instructed to time the cadence of their start in 1-second intervals, for consistency. For this type of start, the dog should be released on the "get set" cue. The dogs need to be crossing the line on "go."

Timekeeping

Timekeeping is a very important part of running a Flyball team. As important as it is to practice the separate parts of Flyball training apart from the whole, it is necessary to practice running the team as a team to get times for recordkeeping purposes.

Your team will need a stopwatch that is capable of recording lap times or splits. One that has recall of up to five lap times is good. There is one available from Seiko that will record and remember up to 100 times. It can even be connected to a printer later for a paper readout of the times. Choose the stopwatch that best suits your needs and your budget.

The timekeeper needs to stand at the starting line and begin the race with the usual, "Ready, set, go" cadence, spaced one second apart. The watch must be started on "go," whether or not the dog has reached the line yet. Having a slow start will affect the team's overall time, so slow starts must be taken into consideration when timing.

When the first dog's nose crosses the starting line on the way back, the timer hits the lap button. Again, it doesn't matter where the second dog is in relation to the first. If the second dog has a late pass, then it will be added to his overall time, not the first dog's time. The time is always stopped on the returning dog's nose. After hitting the lap buttons for all four dogs and stopping the watch, the timer will need to press the recall button to have the individual, or "lap," times displayed one at a time.

Recordkeeping

Keeping individual records, as well as team times, is very important. You will want to know which dog is the fastest, in what position and at what jump height. In addition to doing this at practices, you should also keep records at competitions. Many dogs run faster at real competitions, so if you want to know how fast your team will run at an upcoming tournament, look at your statistics from other tournaments.

After each heat, the timer reads off the dogs' individual times to the scribe, who notes them in the team's statistic sheet.

In addition to the times, it is important to record the conditions at the race. For instance, you will want to note the jump height, ground conditions, length of run-back area and any other pertinent information. Also, if the dog fumbles the ball, goes out around a jump or has a bad pass or other problem that could affect her individual time, it should be noted. Sometimes at a tournament, for example, there will be a flag in the opponent's lane, and our team will deliberately ease up on their passes, resulting in slower times. We have a little notation that indicates "late on purpose" so that the captain or statistician can take this into consideration when calculating the dog's speed for comparison with other team dogs. You will not want to average the times that are abnormally slow due to fumbles, box malfunctions or other problems unless the dog is a habitual fumbler (which needs to be taken into consideration when setting your teams).

1 Karli 5	Dog's Choice Chargers Sparks Team	Tournament Peoria	Date 12-1-96	Division 2	Breakout 20.0
2 Wile E. 6	Captain Lonnie Loader Mike Evaluator Michelle Timer Sheri	Scribe Pam	Runner___		Best time 20.8
3 Koda					
4 Willie					

		Team		Dogs	Time	Tpt	Fpt	Dog 1	Dog 2	Dog 3	Dog 4	Rerun	Total	Notes
1	Heat 1	of 4b	vs Hawkeye	①②③④5 6	20.23	W L T	25	521	497	492	522		20.32	late start
2	Heat 2	of 4b	vs "	①②③④5 6	20.54	W L T	25	512	508	503	527		20.50	
3	Heat 3	of 4b	vs "	①②③④5 6	Breakout	W D T	1	0	479	510	490	519	19.98	Breakout
4	Heat 1	of 50	vs BC Boom	①②③④5 6	20.91	W L T		25	542	538	519	520	21.17	
5	Heat 2	of 50	vs "	①②③④5 6	20.96	W L T		25	521	508	523	534	20.86	
6	Heat 3	of 50	vs "	①②③④5 6	21.44	W L T	1	25	563	510	527	615	22.15	Willie H
7	Heat 1	of 60	vs Hurdlin	①②③④5 6	32.90	W D T		0	527	550	855	Koda		Koda FJ"
8	Heat 2	of 60	vs "	①②③④5 6	21.75	W L T		25	538	585	495	554	21.72	
9	Heat 3	of 60	vs "	①②③④5 6	20.87	W L T	1	25	500	501	524	523		
10	Heat 1	of 6b	vs Ballistics	①2 3 ④5 6	22.23	W D T		25						Wile C, L (traffic problem)
11	Heat 2	of 6b	vs "	①2 3 ④5 6	20.77	W D T		25	no time					
12	Heat 3	of 6b	vs "	①2 3 ④5 6	21.23	W L T	1	25						
13	Heat 1	of 74	vs Flashback 2	①2 3 ④5 6	21.94	W D T		25	524	545	511	617	21.97	
14	Heat 2	of 74	vs "	①2 3 ④5 6	21.77	W D T		25	508	514	525	624	21.71	
15	Heat 3	of 74	vs "	①2 3 ④5 6	29.50	W D T	1	1	513	519	741	533	880	29.47 Koda F Willie E
16	Heat 1	of 88	vs Paw Power	①2 3 ④5 6	20.97	W D T		25	530	520	523	547	21.07	
17	Heat 2	of 88	vs "	①2 3 ④5 6	26.79	W D T		5	538	561	515	535	540	26.89 Willie E
18	Heat 3	of 88	vs "	①2 3 ④5 6	21.36	W L T	1	25	548	553	517	556	21.74	
19	Heat __	of __	vs ___	1 2 3 4 5 6		W L T								
20	Heat __	of __	vs ___	1 2 3 4 5 6		W L T								
21	Heat __	of __	vs ___	1 2 3 4 5 6		W L T								
22	Heat __	of __	vs ___	1 2 3 4 5 6		W L T								
23	Heat __	of __	vs ___	1 2 3 4 5 6		W L T								
24	Heat __	of __	vs ___	1 2 3 4 5 6		W L T								
25	Heat __	of __	vs ___	1 2 3 4 5 6		W L T								
26	Heat __	of __	vs ___	1 2 3 4 5 6		W L T								
27	Heat __	of __	vs ___	1 2 3 4 5 6		W L T								
28	Heat __	of __	vs ___	1 2 3 4 5 6		W L T								
29	Heat __	of __	vs ___	1 2 3 4 5 6		W L T								
30	Heat __	of __	vs ___	1 2 3 4 5 6		W L T								
31	Heat __	of __	vs ___	1 2 3 4 5 6		W L T								
32	Heat __	of __	vs ___	1 2 3 4 5 6		W L T								
33	Heat __	of __	vs ___	1 2 3 4 5 6		W L T								
34	Heat __	of __	vs ___	1 2 3 4 5 6		W L T								
35	Heat __	of __	vs ___	1 2 3 4 5 6		W L T								
36	Heat __	of __	vs ___	1 2 3 4 5 6		W L T								

Notes: F=fumble J=no jump B=no ball E=early pass (flag) L=late pass i=interference H=flag in other lane (held dog back on purpose)

An example of the sheet my team uses to record individual dogs' times and team times. The statistician notes the race number and the competition's name, circles the numbers of the dogs that raced, circles win, lose or tie and records the individual times in the columns for dogs 1–4. Total time is recorded to the right of that. In the last column, it should be noted if there was a fumble or a late pass. The column labeled "Time" is for recording the official times so the team will know how many Flyball title points each dog will receive. The "Tpt" column is for keeping track of tournament points.

	A	B	C	D	E	F	G	H	I	J	K
1	RALLY	4.67	4.30	10"	SLAMMERS	37	FOURTH	KARLI	AMPERES	OUTSIDE	NEW BOX
2	ELLI	4.69	4.44	10"	PAWBUSTERS	16	SECOND	BRITE	AMPERES	OUTSIDE	OLD BOX
3	BRITE	4.80	4.51	10"	SLAMMERS	40	SECOND	JET	AMPERES	OUTSIDE	NEW BOX
4	SNAP!	4.84	4.39	10"	SLAMMERS	35	FIRST		SPARKS	OUTSIDE	NEW BOX
5	TESS	4.85	4.45	8"	SLAMMERS	30	FIRST		MEGAVOLTS	OUTSIDE	NEW BOX
6	ELI	4.90	4.67	8"	RUDE DOGS	24	FIRST		SPARKS	INSIDE	OLD BOX
7	KARLI	5.05	4.80	10"	SLAMMERS	35	THIRD	BRITE	AMPERES	OUTSIDE	NEW BOX
8	GUS	5.12	4.67	8"	RUDE DOGS	25	THIRD	WEASEL	SPARKS	INSIDE	OLD BOX
9	KODA	5.26	4.86	8"	SLAMMERS	35	SECOND	TESS	MEGAVOLTS	OUTSIDE	NEW BOX
10	GATOR	5.34	4.95	10"	SLAMMERS	5	SECOND	SNAP	SPARKS	OUTSIDE	NEW BOX
11	SAVVY	5.48	4.99	10"	SLAMMERS	33	SECOND	SNAP	SPARKS	OUTSIDE	NEW BOX
12	STORMY	5.54	4.82	10"	SLAMMERS	34	THIRD	SAVVY	SPARKS	OUTSIDE	NEW BOX
13	WILE E	5.54	4.94	8"	SLAMMERS	33	THIRD	KODA	MEGAVOLTS	OUTSIDE	NEW BOX
14	COPY	6.54	6.09	8"	RUDE DOGS	10	FOURTH	CAPER	LIVEWIRES	INSIDE	OLD BOX
15	KOKO	6.93	6.49	8"	RUDE DOGS	17	THIRD	TESS	LIVEWIRES	INSIDE	OLD BOX
16											
17											
18											
19											
20											
21	JET	5.03	4.46	10"	SLAMMERS	40	FIRST		AMPERES	OUTSIDE	NEW BOX
22	WILLIE	5.80	5.36	10"	SLAMMERS	35	FOURTH	STORMY	SPARKS	OUTSIDE	NEW BOX
23	WEASEL	6.96	6.61	8"	RUDE DOGS	24	SECOND	ELI	SPARKS	INSIDE	OLD BOX
24	CAPER	7.10	5.62	8"	SLAMMERS	34	FOURTH	WILE E	MEGAVOLTS	OUTSIDE	NEW BOX

This is a database printout of how I analyze the information from the tournament racing sheets. The dogs are seeded by sorting the database on the "average time" field. The data shown here was compiled over several tournaments attended in 1994. Columns indicate dog's name; average time; best time; height at which best time was achieved; tournament at which best time was recorded; number of races averaged to arrive at average time; running position; dog passed; team on which dog ran; inside or outside tournament; and which box was used. All of these factors would come into consideration when evaluating these results.

Chapter 8

Building a
Team

I f you think you would like to become involved in the sport of Flyball, there may be a team near you to join. With Flyball teams spread out all over the country, many participants drive more than an hour to get to team practices. If you live in an area even farther from a practice than this, you may have to get your own team started. All you need is several more people who share your enthusiasm for the sport.

I get many of my new "recruits" from the Obedience classes I teach throughout the year. But sometimes people come to the team because they hear about it from a friend, or they see an article about our team in the newspaper. Sometimes, I have been approached at a local Flyball tournament by spectators who think their dog would be great at this sport. Regardless of where the prospective members come from, you cannot go any further by yourself without building a team. Here are some suggestions for you to attract potential teammates.

Offer to do a demonstration for your local Obedience club. Even if you are not affiliated with the club, they may agree to let you provide the demonstration as an educational event for a club meeting or as lunchtime entertainment at their dog show or fun match. Have flyers with you stating your address and phone number and mentioning that you are looking for other enthusiasts to join your team (no experience necessary).

This same advice goes for county fairs, hometown celebrations or just about anywhere else crowds of people might be apt to see your demonstration and think, "Gee, my dog would do that!" It doesn't even have to be a dog-related activity (but it helps). If you are fresh out of ideas, here are some more possible audiences for you:

- Sports competitions (halftime entertainment)

- Nursing home demonstrations (the audience may not have dogs, but you could get a write-up in the local newspaper, which dog owners will read)

- Humane Society fund-raisers (lots of dog people here)

- Dog events (Frisbee® competitions, Agility trials, dog camps)

- Fun runs (while entrants are racing, the fans and spectators need something to do)

- Other charity events (walkathons, carnivals)

- Parades (yes, you can demonstrate Flyball while walking in a parade!)

Always have flyers containing recruitment information with you when you do these demonstrations. Be sure to let the local media know about the demonstration. Free publicity is always a good way to get in the public eye. And, don't forget to put flyers up in local pet supply shops.

Leadership Styles

It won't be long before you have a few other interested people, and you've got yourself a team. It would be a good idea to plan ahead for the style of leadership you plan to use for the team. Many people favor a club-type format when they first start out. Most of the teams I know that have started out as clubs have now broken off and use various other types of organization. A monarchy actually works best. People know what to expect. They know their ideas are welcomed and will be considered, but that one individual makes the final decision. If the participants know from the start that the organization is going to have one person calling all of the shots, they don't tend to get upset when things don't go their way.

Another advantage to "owning" the team is that all of the equipment belongs to you, preventing arguments as to who gets what in the event that your team ever splits up. This is just my personal experience. Everyone has to use what works best for his or her own team.

Obedience training clubs don't like to sacrifice floor time for a Flyball team's regular practice when they could have paying students using the building instead. But training clubs don't mind when your team hosts a Flyball tournament and adds several hundred dollars to the club treasury. They may get upset, however, when you want to use some of that money to buy your team members new uniforms. After hearing people say, "but this is an Obedience club," over and over again, you start thinking you should move along and have a separate organization.

Getting Organized

When you have enough people together to start calling yourself a team, you have to think about what you want to call yourselves. There are over 400 teams in competition, and most of them have really cute, catchy names. You can consult the NAFA teams list to make sure that the name you have chosen is not duplicating someone else's. Think hard and come up with something original. Just when I think that all of the cute names have been taken already, a new team comes along with one of those ingenious names that makes you say, "Why didn't I think of that?"

Your team will also have to make some decisions on a few other important issues. What type of Flyball box you will use for competition and what your uniforms will look like are things you should discuss. The team will also need to find a suitable practice location and decide how to handle trainees and new members. Sooner or later, your team will have to have some rules and guidelines to keep things in order and flowing smoothly.

Team Bonding

It's always fun to be part of a Flyball team and play this great sport, but some things can make your team an even more closely-knit unit. When you enjoy time with your team members outside the realm of Flyball training, it helps to create a bond among members and makes everything you do together more fun. You become like a big family.

One of the things that promotes cohesiveness is what I call the "pack feeding frenzy." Eating is an activity we all enjoy, and a team can think of many ways to turn simple eating into a team bonding experience.

First, there is the Thursday night, post-practice dining ritual when everyone stops at a restaurant on the way home from practice to eat, drink and be merry. Next, there is the "surprise, it's someone's birthday" party. It could be a birthday or any other noteworthy occasion that possibly warrants the appearance of cake and other goodies at practice (or at a tournament). Of course, there's the annual picnic (or beach party, barbecue, beer fest or any other excuse to get together for fun and merriment). Then there are the tournament potlucks, where each member brings something indescribably delicious and a big feast is spread out at the tournament for lunch in the team's crating area. All of these foodfests are combined with lots of joking, storytelling and other tomfoolery, of course.

This is where the teams "hang out" at a tournament. Each team has its own crating area staked out where the members gather to rest, eat, care for the dogs and plan strategies for the races to come.

Eating isn't the only thing that bonds a team together. There are also the practical jokes and other fun things that make you feel like soul mates with your fellow team members. Taking a team picture is a nice thing to do at tournaments or other get-togethers. A team trip is also a lot of fun. Some of the extracurricular activities I have enjoyed with fellow team members include bicycling around Mackinac Island (dogs included), going to a water slide park, camping, shopping and getting the dogs on a television commercial.

Sportsmanship

It should go without saying that you and your team must conduct yourselves in a sportsmanlike manner whenever you are in public. Think about how you speak to your teammates, your dog, the officials and the opposing teams. What does it look like to someone who has never seen this activity before? Would they think you were treating your dog like a machine? Would they see you speaking abruptly to a judge? Would they see you lose your temper at a teammate? You must always be cognizant of what your actions look like to other people. We certainly don't want our sport banned because poor treatment of animals is exhibited.

I have seen one Flyball participant who held her dog by the tail. It didn't seem to bother the dog any, but to the average pet owner, it seemed "cruel." She was asked to stop because of the negative image it was giving to the spectators.

When I race, I don't even hold my dogs by the collars. They pull and strain so hard they would constantly be choking themselves. I wrap one arm around their mid-section or chest to restrain them, and hang onto the collar for safety.

Etiquette

At a Flyball tournament, in addition to exhibiting good sportsmanship, there are certain ways to conduct yourself that I feel fall more under the category of etiquette.

During a race, keep your dogs, people and balls on your own half of the course. If any of the opponent's balls roll over to your side, it's nice to return them. Keep your own balls in your container—don't let them roll around on the ground to trip on, or to distract the other team's dogs (this can be called interference).

Wait for the judge's decision (after both teams have finished the heat) before clapping for the winning team. Always shake hands with the opposing team's members after a race (this includes box loaders). Congratulate them if it was a win for them, or thank them for congratulating you.

After the racing with that team is finished, grab your stuff and clear the lane as quickly as possible because there will be two other teams coming in for their warm-up time. Often at tournaments, time is critical, so don't lollygag and prevent the other team from taking the field.

Last, but not least, enjoy!

Judge Dave Samuels measures "Casey" while owner, Phyllis O'Brien, helps the dog to hold still. It is important for the dogs to learn to hold still for measuring, for if they refuse measurement, they must automatically jump the maximum jump height of 16".

Chapter 9

Getting into
Competition

The North American Flyball Association

At the time of this writing, the only sanctioned Flyball competitions in North America are held under the auspices of the North American Flyball Association (NAFA). Flyball competition has evolved considerably over the past 12 years; there is already talk of a "World Flyball Association." In this book, I have tried to give an overview of the current procedures. Things could be very different 10 years from now.

The first thing you must do if you intend to race your dog(s) in Flyball competitions is to register with NAFA by applying for a Certified Racing Number (CRN) for each dog. This number will be put on all forms to identify each team and dog. In this way, NAFA keeps track of which dogs race and earn points toward their Flyball titles. To register a dog, contact NAFA, Inc., 1400 W. Devon Ave., Box 512, Chicago, IL 60660. A 24-hour phone service is available at (309) 688-9840. There is a one-time fee ($15, American funds) for registering your dog with NAFA.

When you contact NAFA, ask to subscribe to *The Finish Line*, a publication which lists upcoming tournaments and posts the results of recent tournaments. It also includes a seeding chart, ranking all of the teams currently in competition by best time. In addition, there are articles and advertisements and other items of interest (American funds). Contact Melanie McAvay, Editor, 1002 E. Samuel Ave., Peoria Heights, IL 61614.

NAFA has an official publication, *NAFA News,* which is focused on recent NAFA Board of Directors' meetings, new policies, a column written by the executive director and short articles by Flyball judges. The purpose of this publication is to keep members current on rules and policies and official NAFA business. The *NAFA News* is sent out quarterly to all team delegates. It also posts a list of upcoming sanctioned tournaments and their closing dates.

Preparing for Competition

After you have your dogs registered and have found a tournament you would like to enter, send your money to the tournament director. Sometimes you enter on an official form, and sometimes you just fill out a slip of paper with your team name, contact person and the time you expect your team to run. The tournament director will use this information to seed (rank) your team in a division with other teams of similar speed. It is important that you include an accurate indication of your team's expected times, as your team will be penalized if you run too much faster than the times you submitted. This is to keep teams from "sandbagging" (as described in an earlier chapter) and submitting slower times to be placed in a more favorable bracket (increasing their chances of winning).

Before the tournament, you should have jobs assigned to your team members, and make sure each person knows what is expected. Here are some of the jobs which need to be assigned:

- **Loader:** hopefully the same person with whom the team has practiced

- **Timer:** someone to take individual times for your team

- **Scribe:** the person who helps the timer by recording the times for your team

- **Pass Evaluator:** a line coach who will tell the racers how good their passes were

- **Runner:** someone to stand by and set jumps, go after wayward balls or whatever

- **Ball Shagger:** someone to make sure the balls get picked up and put in the bucket

- **Captain:** the person who makes strategy decisions during the race

- **Video camera operator:** to record the starts and passes for later viewing and evaluation

Your team may not be big enough to have the spare personnel to do most of these jobs. That's okay. Your team will function much better, however, if you do have people doing these jobs. Maybe you can "borrow" a member from another team to help you until you build your team size a little.

Ready, Set, Go!

You should receive a confirmation of entry in the mail at least one week before the tournament. The map and other important information can be copied and distributed to team members at the pre-tournament meeting. Other information in your confirmation will be the starting time, division breakdowns, breakout times and racing schedule. You will have an idea of when you will race and approximately how many races you will run during the weekend. Strategies for the competition, job assignments and other plans should be discussed at the pre-tournament meeting.

Before racing begins on the day of the tournament, you will have an opportunity to have your dogs measured by an official. There will also be a time to allow the judge to inspect boxes. There will probably be a captains' meeting shortly before the start of racing. Any special rules, warm-up or tie-breaking policies or reminders will be announced at the meeting. Be sure to attend the meeting and convey any pertinent information to your team members. You may already have picked up your time sheets from the head table, or you may pick them up at the captains' meeting. You must have your team's time sheets filled out and turned in to the head table before the racing for your division starts.

For your own information, you should keep a duplicate record of the time sheet. This way, you will have your own record of which dogs ran, the official finishing times and the results of each heat (win, lose or tie). From this you can determine how many points each dog should be receiving toward a Flyball title. Also, you will know exactly how many heats each dog raced (in case you use this information to prorate the entry fees of the members). You will also have an idea of what kind of times your team will run at a tournament. Often, dogs run much faster in actual competition. You can use these times when you enter future tournaments with these same dogs.

After each race, the official times will be posted on the chart so that teams can copy down the official race results. This also lets you see the times the other teams are running so you can plan your racing strategy when you run against them. For instance, if you will be up against a team that is running a full 2 seconds faster than yours, you might want to put in one of the back-up dogs to get the title points for those heats since there's no way you are going to beat this team anyway.

A team checks the official times posted on the wall chart at a tournament.

As each race begins, the teams are allowed a warm-up time. How you take advantage of your warm-up depends on your dogs and at what stage in the tournament you are. If you have seasoned dogs and you are undefeated in the double-elimination finals, you will not want to tire your dogs with another warm-up when they may be racing ten times in a row to determine the winner of the division. You may have newer, back-up dogs who won't be racing but who would benefit from the warm-up. During the regular racing, I usually opt to do a restrained Recall to let the dogs know which lane they're in and to remind them to come back fast. Then, if there's time, we run the four dogs as a team, with our passes evaluated.

Before each race, the team warms up the dogs. Restrained Recalls help the dog know which lane he is in, and are only half as tiring as running the whole course. Restrained Recalls also remind the dog that it is his job to come back quickly for his target.

The Race

Immediately prior to the start of each heat, the captain must decide which four dogs will run. He then gives that information to the line judge, so that he can circle the appropriate dogs' numbers on the racing sheet. Make sure you let the judge know if you make substitutions, as only the dogs that are circled on the racing sheet will receive title points for that heat. Also be sure to inform your box loader of the lineup and running order. This is particularly important if you use a smaller-size ball for a little dog, or if you use a box with multiple cups. Make sure your team knows who is running and in what order, making sure that they have found their take-off points on the mat.

Be sure you have a competent individual loading your box for you. If you are shorthanded and just grab any available person to do the job, they will probably make errors. I think it is an unwritten rule that all new boxloaders forget to load the box one time. Of course, it is so embarrassing that it usually doesn't happen a second time, but you may not be able to spare the points the first time. You never know when it will happen. It's just that people get so wrapped up in the game, they forget what they are supposed to do. The loader is the unsung hero of the team. This person is in charge of the Flyball box, and should be able to not only lift and carry it (sometimes they're very heavy), but should have enough of an idea of how it works that he would be able to fix it if it malfunctions. The loader should be familiar with all of the box rules and should know what is required to load the box for each dog on the team.

Racing Formats

Tournament formats can be round robin, double elimination, single elimination or a combination. The total entry of teams is usually broken up into divisions, grouped together by seeding times. Each division will have a "breakout time" of about one second faster than the fastest team's expected time. If a team "breaks out" by running too fast, they lose that heat (even though they might have beaten the other team). If both teams break out, they rerun the race and no title points or tournament points are awarded for that heat.

In a **round-robin** competition, each team in your division will have an opportunity to run against every other team in the division at least once. Tournament points are accumulated by counting wins, and ties are usually broken by looking back at the winner of the head-to-head competition between the two teams in question.

In a **double-** or **single-elimination** competition, teams are placed in a bracket and race until they are beaten. As long as they continue to win, they move up the bracket, but if they lose, they move down to the loser's bracket (in double elimination). In the end, the winner of the loser's bracket gets one more chance to race against the first-place team in the winner's bracket (because a team must be defeated twice to be eliminated).

Some tournament directors opt for a format of round-robin racing on Saturday to determine the seeding for a double-elimination final on Sunday. Wins determine placings at the end of each day, and the placings are allotted points (one point for first, two points for second, etc.). The team with the lowest point total on Sunday is the winner. If there are ties for overall placements, they are broken by various methods, depending on whether or not the tournament is running behind schedule. Ties may be broken with additional racing or by using the team's best time.

When the tournament is over, you will hopefully have had fun, earned lots of title points, made new friends and learned something new. At your team's post-tournament meeting, you can discuss the good and bad aspects of your team's performance, review videotapes, celebrate new titles or achievements and begin planning for how you will do things differently to improve the team's performance in the next tournament.

Flyball Points and Titles

As dogs race in a sanctioned competition, they are earning points with each heat that count toward Flyball titles. The point system is based on team times. For a heat finished in less than 32 seconds, one point is awarded to each of the racing dogs. If the time is less than 28 seconds, five points are earned. Finishing under 24 seconds will rack up 25 points per heat. These points are tallied and kept on record with the North American Flyball Association. When a dog has amassed enough points to earn the next title, NAFA sends a certificate attesting to this.

Titles are based on total points earned. Following is a schedule of the progression of titles available from NAFA, based on this point system:

Total Points	Title	Abbreviation
20	Flyball Dog	FD
100	Flyball Dog Excellent	FDX
500	Flyball Champion	FDCh
1,000	Flyball Master	FM
5,000	Flyball Master Excellent	FMX
10,000	Flyball Master Champion	FMCh
20,000	"Onyx" award	
30,000	Flyball Dog Grand Champion	FDGCh

The point system for the first three basic titles originated in the early days of Flyball, when it was actually quite a challenge to run under 24 seconds. Currently, most teams in competition are well under the 24 second per race range. The titles have also expanded to include those in the range of tens of thousands of points. The Onyx award was originated to honor dogs that have earned the ultimate challenge of achieving 20,000 points. This seemed like quite a stretch at its inception, but as Flyball dogs continue to earn points, we see dogs that are reaching the 30,000-point mark and are still going strong.

The Onyx Plaque

The Onyx award is named for the first dog to reach the 20,000 point mark. The first dog to do this was a Doberman, owned by regional director Clyde Moore. Onyx came to live with Clyde when she was a year old. Her owners wanted to get rid of Onyx because she barked, and Clyde saw the ad in the paper. When Clyde first saw Onyx, she was diving off the front porch of the people's mobile home, chasing after a squeaky toy. She snatched up the toy and flew back to the porch, gave the toy to the owner and began leaping up and down, begging the owner to throw it again. Clyde had this feeling that Onyx would be a great Flyball dog. He was right.

Onyx was only 48 pounds at the time Clyde took her. She looked like a bag of bones. She is seven years old now, and while still sleek, she is not a bag of bones anymore. Clyde says that Onyx never tires of games that involve retrieving. She will play until Clyde is too tired to throw anymore.

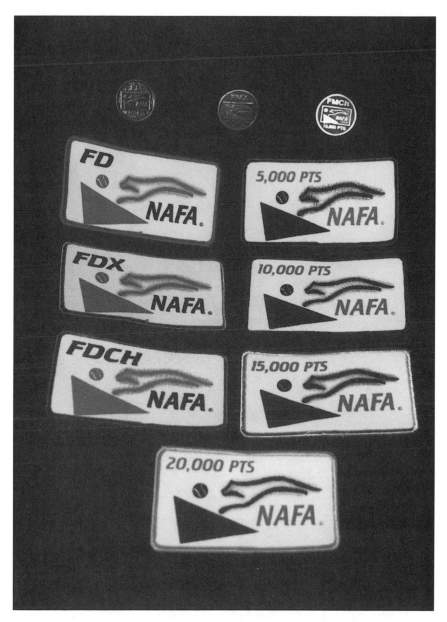

Patches and pins that are available from NAFA for earning Flyball title points.

Onyx was a natural, and caught on to Flyball immediately. She currently has accumulated over 40,000 points.

Clyde says that Onyx has been an exceptional dog. She has been a wonderful friend, companion and canine athlete who has entertained many people all over North America.

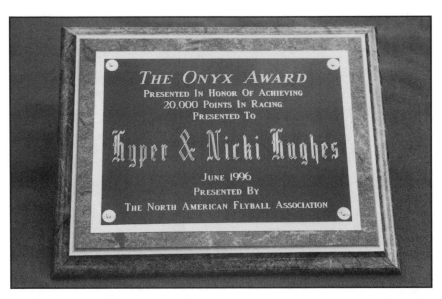

The Onyx Award is a special plaque given to dogs that achieve a total of 20,000 title points.

"Onyx," owned by Clyde Moore, was the first dog to reach the 20,000-point mark.

Chapter 10

Hosting a Tournament

Hosting a tournament of your own can be a fun and worthwhile experience. It is also a lot of work. You will need a group of people to help with putting on the tournament, and you will probably benefit from assigning committees to handle various aspects of the job. That way no one has to do all of the work alone.

Choose a Site

The first thing you will want to do is locate a suitable site for your tournament. Many schools do not like to rent their gymnasiums to Flyball teams because of the potential damage to the hardwood floors. Even if your club has access to enough rubber matting to fully cover the racing area, there is always the chance that someone will walk a dog across an unprotected area and scratch the floor. Dogs don't usually "walk" through a room in which Flyball competition is taking place—they try to drag their owners out there to play!

Fairgrounds are good locations to hold tournaments. They usually have large buildings with cement floors that can be covered with mats. Dirt floors like those found in riding arenas or sheep barns are not good for Flyball competitions. While the dirt allows for great shock absorption, the dogs sink in a little when they land and their jumping could be off a little because of this. In addition, after several runs you will notice a deep trench forming. When people do use these kinds of buildings, they are advised to lay down sod, like they would mats, in the racing lanes and around the boxes. In addition, lots of additional sod must be kept on hand for patching the ruts left by dogs running over and over the same spot all day—especially right in front of the box. There also has to be some method of anchoring the sod so that it doesn't flip up, bunch up or slide. Dirt floor conditions are workable, but they are not the best.

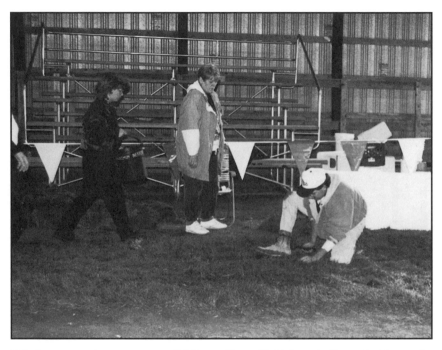

This tournament was run on a dirt floor with sod laid down in the racing lanes. As the dogs pulverized the sod, pushing off at the start or screeching to a stop at the box, the sod was repaired or replaced and re-anchored. Note the extra rolls of sod around the sidelines.

If the climate and weather are agreeable, you can host an outdoor tournament. If you have an outdoor tournament on a hot and humid day, be sure to have a wading pool where the dogs can cool down after racing. Also, you will want to caution all competitors not to allow their dogs to jump in the water right before running as this will wet down the racing lane and make the grass slippery for the other dogs to run on. In addition, if there is not plenty of shade available, you will need to mention this in your premium list or flyer so that people can bring their own screen tents or sunshades for the dogs.

Sometimes you can get involved with some other group hosting an activity, like a dog fun day or pet expo, that would be happy to have Flyball racing as an added attraction. By going in with another group, you can save a lot of money on building rental and sometimes get a really nice site for your competition.

Pick a Date

After you are sure you have a workable location, you will need to pin down a date. Remember that Flyball people are often also involved in Obedience, Herding, Agility or other dog activities, so try not to schedule your event to conflict with any of these other competitions if you want to get a good turnout.

Decide if a one- or two-day format would work best. If you are in a remote area with very few teams, you can get a lot of racing done in just one day. If, on the other hand, you are expecting 100 or more entries, you will need the maximum amount of time possible to give everyone a fair amount of racing. People don't want to drive five hours to race three times and go home!

If you have more than about 70 teams entering in one weekend, you will have to use a two-ring format to allow enough time for all the racing to take place. This means that you will need two judges, two sets of jumps and backdrops, two sets of lights and two compliments of table people, announcers, box judges and line judges. If your building is large enough, this is not a problem. As a matter of fact, if you live in an area with a lot of Flyball teams, it can be the most effective way of holding a tournament. You can take entries from more teams, and each team will still have plenty of racing.

If you are not able to provide the personnel, the time or the space to run this type of a tournament, you may want to opt for a limited-entry tournament so that you know you will have only a certain number of teams in attendance.

A **limited entry** is only slightly different from an unlimited tournament. You would have to submit your request for sanctioning further in advance of the tournament (120 days) to allow everyone an equal chance to get their entry in. You would also not be able to allow the teams to run the same dogs in a multibreed division and the regular division at the same tournament unless entries were not filled up.

Entries are taken on a first-come basis except in the case of multiple entries of the same club. If the entries have not closed and a new team wants to get in, a single entry from a different club can bump a second

This tournament was the first tournament to use a two-ring setup. The arrangement was set up to control traffic. Only one judge officiated, and went back and forth between the rings. The racing teams were able to get their boxes out, set the jump heights and warm up their dogs while the other lane was competing. When the judge changed lanes, all he had to do was start the race.

This photo of a two-ring setup shows a finish line view of the four lanes of racing. The starting dogs in the near ring have been let go. The green light has not come on yet, but it will be lit by the time the dogs' noses get to the start. The pass evaluators watch the line to give feedback to the teams. Line judges watch the lights for a false start. In the far ring, the teams wait for the starting dog to reach the timing point so they can let go of their second dogs. In the far lane, the returning Border Collie is just touching down between the two middle jumps. Right on cue, Kathie Duguid (in front of Judge Kevin Hughes) is just letting go of her Border Collie, "Lady." The two dogs should meet at the start/finish line for a perfect pass.

entry from the same team of an already entered club. In other words, no single team will be shut out because another club entered five teams and filled the entry.

Decide if you are going to offer a **non-regular division** in addition to your **regular divisions**. You will need to note this information on your application for sanction and on your flyers. Many teams like to enter both divisions, if possible. Multibreed is a non-regular class, as are Pee Wee and Veterans classes. At this time, the rules do not define Pee Wee or Veterans classes, so if you wanted to request that your Pee Wee division be for any dog jumping 10 inches or less, or your Veterans class be for dogs seven years of age or older, you could request permission to offer the class as such.

After you have decided on the date, location and whether you want a limited or unlimited tournament, you can hire the judges. Ask what the judge's fees are and whether or not the judge will require a night's lodging. For a list of NAFA-approved judges, see the NAFA Rules and Policies book.

Choose a closing date far enough in advance of your tournament so that it will allow you to plan your format and get the information back out into the mail for the teams that have entered. Sometimes the mail between the United States and Canada is slow, so leave several weeks' time at the very least.

When you have all of this information together, you can send in your application to host a NAFA-sanctioned Flyball competition. If your application is approved, your tournament date will appear in the Flyball publications so that the teams will know of your upcoming tournament. You may choose to distribute flyers in addition to this.

Where Do You Go for Help After Your Tournament Has Been Approved?

Your regional director (R.D.) is there to help you. Don't be afraid to call on the R.D. for any help you may need in planning the tournament, especially if you are inexperienced. The R.D. will help you work out your seeding schedule, racing format and division breaks. Or, if you are capable of doing this yourself, the R.D. will check it over and give approval. The R.D. will also make sure that the official timing light system gets shipped to you in time for your tournament, and will help you understand how to set it up and operate it.

In addition to your regional director, you can find much help in the NAFA Rules and Policies booklet. In Appendix C of that booklet, you will find form C.4—the Tournament Checklist. This handy form will help you plan everything for your tournament, from setting up the committee to turning in the records to NAFA.

Deciding on a Format

The racing format you choose will depend on the number of teams that will be racing and the time you have available. If you only have the site from 9:00 AM to 5:00 PM, you will be limited to less than eight hours of racing. In this amount of time, you could do four divisions of six teams each, using double elimination (40–44 races). Or, in a round-robin format, you would have time for three divisions of six teams each (45 races). The problem is that in double elimination, each team is guaranteed only two races. With the round-robin format, each team will race every other team, ensuring five races. Teams want to race at least five times after traveling great distances, in some cases, to attend your tournament.

The NAFA Rules and Policies booklet has all of this information broken down for you in Appendix F—Racing Schedules. It has examples of how many hours are required to judge so many races, depending on which racing format you use. It also maps out the schedule of which teams race each other, and in which order. After seeding the teams, all you have to do is type up the schedule using the teams' names instead of their seeding numbers.

Inviting Spectators (or Not)

Whether or not you open up your tournament to the public is a matter of preference. A Flyball tournament has great spectator appeal. Revenue for your group can also be accrued by charging admission to your event. On the other hand, you may have to deal with advertising, ticket sales, concessions, programs and cleaning up after an event with a large audience. You also have to think about keeping the public out of the Flyball teams' crating areas. There are many pros and cons to having spectators at your event. Each host has to weigh out the benefits and decide for themselves.

Entry Confirmation

When the entries have closed and you have seeded the teams and decided on a format, you will need to print up all of this information to send back to the entered teams. Include the following information in your confirmation and welcome letter:

- Directions to the tournament site
- Crating information (location, shade, limited space, restrictions, loading zones)
- Captains' meeting time
- Dog measuring time
- Judges
- Racing format
- Division breakdowns (list the teams racing in each division)
- Scheduled times for each division's racing
- Tie-breaking format
- Building rules or special restrictions
- Food availability
- Hotels or campgrounds in the area

The more information you provide for the teams, the fewer unhappy people you will have.

Setting up the Course

The first thing to do when setting up your course is to position the Electronic Judging System (EJS). Place it in the center, between the two lanes. The electric cords will have to be run under the matting. The best place to do this is just beyond the first jump as it is very rare that a dog will land in that area. Be sure to tape down all of the wires carefully. Position your head table so that the workers there can easily let the judge know that the EJS has been reset between heats. Keep in mind that there may be several team members (pass evaluators, scribes, timers, captains) standing directly in back of the line judge. Some host teams choose to tape off a square around the line judge's chair so that he will not be hindered by people crowding all around him.

The overall dimensions for the Flyball racing course are a minimum of 30 feet by 90 feet. This allows for a minimum 29-foot run-back area and at least 7 feet behind the boxes.

- The actual Flyball racing course measures 51 feet from starting line to the front of the box.

- The first jump is 6 feet from the starting line.

- The jumps are 10 feet apart.

- The box is 15 feet past the last jump.

- The lanes must be at least 10 feet apart and no more than 20 feet apart.

- Backstops measuring at least 2 feet high must surround the two boxes so that the balls don't bounce too far out of bounds.

- Mats must be put down to allow for traction in the entire box area, from the last jump to the backstops. The actual racing lanes have to have only one mat covering the actual lane, but if extra mats are available, it is good to place an additional mat on either side of the racing lanes. The run-back area, starting from the last jump, must be matted on either side of the main racing lane to allow for dogs to come off to one side or the other.

When you lay out your course (usually the day before the tournament), you will want to make sure the racing rings meet specifications. There are teams that will check your measurements and let you know if something is $1/8$-inch off, so try to be meticulous. If you are using a gymnasium, you can use the lines on the floor to help you keep your mats straight and your lanes parallel. Make absolutely sure that your two starting lines are exactly in line and plumb, then measure everything from the starting line.

The best way to mark your course is by putting down duct tape and marking it with permanent marker. Measure from each side of the racing lane as you place the marks for each jump on the mat. To mark the correct position of the Flyball box, lay the tape where the front edge of the box should line up. The starting line tape should be placed so that the edge nearest the run-back area is the actual start. This way, a handler knows that if his foot touches any part of the tape, he is over the line. Some teams like to put down a "warning line" 3 feet back from the actual starting line so that careless handlers do not inadvertently stick arms or legs over the line in the air and trigger the lighting system, causing a red light to come on, resulting in a flag.

In addition to marking the course, you may want to mark the run-back area so that the racing teams will not have to. Each team has unique and individual marks that they use as take-off points for their team. If you let the teams put their own measurements down, it can get confusing. Not all teams measure from the start line. Some measure back from the first jump, so you might have a mark on the floor labeled 26 feet, which is really a 20-foot mark. Also, it can get pretty congested out there with numerous teams each trying to measure and mark the floor. Lastly, the measurements might not be as precise as they would be if one person carefully measured out each mark from the same exact spot on the start line.

Final Preparation

As you prepare for the day of your tournament, make sure that everything is in order. Go over your checklist to make sure you have not forgotten anything. Make sure that you have all of the forms, signs, manpower and equipment you will need.

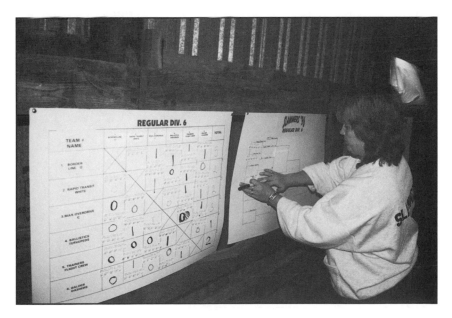

An official from the head table posts the results of the last race on the wall chart so that the competitors can get the official times for their team (and for their competition).

You will need time sheets (form C.2) for all the teams in competition. You will also need a form to record the official times from the Electronic Judging System. You can do this on a regular sheet of notebook paper, but I have made up a form on my computer to make this easier. This form stays at the head table. It will have all of the times from all of the races in case paperwork is lost or a posted time accidentally comes off the board.

You will also need the charts or brackets, which will go up on the wall for posting the results of each race. These can be hand-drawn on poster board, or they can be drawn up and produced in large size on blueprint paper if you have access to the materials. Address labels make good stickers for posting times onto these charts. You can even run them through the computer first to imprint them with race numbers and blank lines, along with "w l t" for win, lose or tie, under each blank line. It is also a nice touch to provide $8^{1}/_{2}$- by 11-inch copies of the charts or double-elimination brackets for each team to keep in their area to follow along with the racing.

Make sure you have enough people at the head table. Recording the racing times, resetting the clock, posting the official results, changing the race number board, getting the next time sheets ready for the judges, announcing races and answering questions are all functions of the head table people. Three to six people should be there to ensure efficiency.

The head table is kept quite busy, and everyone must constantly be on the ball. Times need be written down after each race and the EJS reset, the judge must be notified of any break outs, the line judges should be given the racing sheets for the appropriate next two teams that will be racing, announcements must be made and times must be posted.

With the new breakout rule, you should have a method of informing the judge if one of the teams breaks out. At a recent tournament I attended, the head table had a stick sign made of neon yellow poster board with the words "Break Out" printed on it. In the future, someone will probably figure out how to add policing of breakout times to the function of the EJS equipment. It would be great to have a siren and flashing blue light going off when the EJS senses a recorded time that is under the breakout time (which would be somehow pre-entered into the system before each division).

Be sure to have people available to give relief time to the table people and judges, allowing them time to eat lunch and have some breaks. If you are short on people, you can sometimes get volunteers from the competing teams to step in for you if they are not racing in that particular division. At every tournament there are usually enough other experienced head judges, line judges and box judges who would not mind stepping in for a while to give someone a break or to cover in an emergency.

Your "Laundry List"

Equipment consists of more than just the necessities for the racing area. Don't forget the pooper scoopers, baggies, extra trash cans, paper towels and disinfectant for clean-up. If you are going to have an announcer, make sure the equipment is in place and functioning. If you are going to play the national anthem at the beginning of the competition, you will need a flag, a tape player and a copy of the music. Anthem music can be found at your local library. A coffee pot, dolly, first-aid kit and extra push-brooms are usually good to have on hand, as are tape, scissors, lots of pens, pencils and markers, extra poster board, blank paper and string. Don't forget the 16 or more rolls of duct tape it will take to hold down the mats.

The day of your tournament will be hectic. Don't be discouraged if you receive complaints. It's hard to please every person at each tournament. Do the best you can and try to plan ahead to foresee any potential problems before they arise. When the tournament is over, you will feel a sense of accomplishment due to all of your hard work and effort. If you feel there were problem areas, make a list of what went wrong and try to make a point of improving your next tournament.

When everything is over, you need to fill out the paperwork that must be sent in to NAFA. You have 30 days in which to get it in without a fine. Before sending in the information, make sure that the time sheets have all been filled out correctly. Check to see that all dogs' names have a CRN number or they will not receive Flyball points. Make sure that each race has four dogs' numbers circled, and either a time or a "No Finish" (NF) is recorded for each race. Fill out the Tournament Results Form (C.6) and send it with all of the original time sheets to NAFA headquarters along with the necessary fees ($15 per team entered). GOOD LUCK!

Chapter 11

Preparing *a* **Future** **Flyball** **Star**

Puppy Selection

All Flyball training should start out the same. Whether you are teaching the family pet the fundamentals of the sport or raising a future Flyball champion, you need to go through the same steps. As people have learned through experience, there are dogs who you can train to run Flyball, and there are dogs who are "born" for the sport. Either one can be a successful Flyball competitor. When the sport of Flyball was new, many of us just trained our family pets to play Flyball. We had a lot of fun, but didn't break any speed records. Now, those of us who live and breathe for the sport of Flyball carefully choose dogs that we feel will excel at the sport. You need to select the right puppy and use the proper training technique if you want a truly great Flyball dog.

The most proficient Flyball dogs tend to come from the herding and sporting groups. These dogs possess an intensity for chasing and fetching things, which makes them a natural for the sport. The high-energy dogs from these groups are the Border Collie, Labrador Retriever, Shetland Sheepdog and Golden Retriever. These breeds are seen in large numbers in competitive Flyball racing. Other breeds with good potential are any of the fast, sleek breeds of medium size, providing they have high energy and an intense desire to chase and retrieve balls. Doberman Pinschers are a good example in this category. Terriers are good candidates; they are muscular, agile and energetic. American Staffordshire Terriers and Jack Russell Terriers are different-sized terrier types popular in the sport.

Currently, the most popular breed for Flyball competition is the Border Collie. These dogs have limitless energy, they have the ability to move at great speed, they are agile and their passion for tennis balls is relentless. They will fetch a ball all day long, and would rather play fetch than eat. They can become so obsessed with fetching games that, in an area devoid of anything resembling a dog toy or a ball, they will resort to bringing you a Popsicle stick, a rolled up gum wrapper, a teeny tiny twig, a rock or anything that they think they might be able to get you to throw for them . . . repeatedly . . . ad nauseum! Keep this in mind when you consider getting a Border Collie. They are "high-maintenance" companions—not in grooming or feeding, but by the fact that their high intelligence demands that you give them a lot of attention. This is not a dog to get with the idea that you can tie him out on a chain in the backyard, or keep him cooped up in a kennel all day. Their minds are always challenging you to come up with new ways to keep them entertained. This is not a breed content to sleep at your feet while you watch television.

Border Collies are happy to play fetching games all day long. *Terry Ryan*

After you have selected the breed you feel is right for your needs, you should look at the background or bloodlines of the puppy you are considering. Flyball racing puts a lot of physical demands on a dog. You will want to make sure that the puppy comes from lines free from genetic conditions that would cause problems or end a Flyball career prematurely. Make sure that the parents have been x-rayed for bone problems, checked for eye diseases and have normal hearing. Avoid purchasing a dog from lines that may be likely to produce hip dysplasia, osteochondritis, seizures, vision problems or deafness.

When you have found a litter that seems physically sound, test the puppies individually for their willingness to retrieve. Puppies begin retrieving naturally at a young age (seven to eight weeks) and a puppy already showing an aptitude for fetching games should be easy to teach to be ball-crazy. Ask to see the mother or both parents if the sire is also on the premises. If the sire is owned by someone else, get as much information as you can about him, and contact the dog's owner.

This is what sold me on my first Border Collie. When I went in to see the puppies, the sire ran over to me and said, "Hi! Are you going to sit on the floor there? Would you mind throwing my ball for me a few hundred times?" I fell in love with that dog, and hoped that my puppy would grow up to be just like her father. She did. She's wonderful. I loved "Karli" so much, I went back and got "Wile E. Collie," Karli's full brother from a repeat breeding several years later. My newest puppy, "Koda," is from dogs with Herding, Obedience and Flyball backgrounds. He is also a "great-nephew" of Karli and Wile E. I found a good line that has been successful for me, and I stayed with it. None of my three Border Collies showed any great desire to get the ball at an early age. Temperament and coat color were the two most important factors to me at the time. I was gambling on the puppies growing up to show an interest in the ball later, like their ball-crazy parents. They did.

Ball Play

After you have acquired your new puppy, you can get started on ball training right away. If you have other dogs that already play Flyball, or like the ball, do not try to teach the puppy when they are around. They will beat the puppy to the ball every time, or take the ball away from the puppy, making ball playing very frustrating for the pup.

If the puppy is too small to hold a tennis ball in his mouth, you can use any type of smaller ball. Try to use a lightweight ball, or one that moves slowly, when introducing the puppy to retrieving. Remember that a puppy's motor skills are still developing and they cannot track fast-moving objects easily.

Begin by rolling the ball, rather than tossing it. Go to a quiet place, like the hallway, and sit on the floor with the puppy, just the two of you. Roll the ball down the hall. The only place for the pup to go with the ball, once he gets it, is back toward you. At this stage, even if the puppy is enjoying the retrieving, most pups will not yet equate bringing the ball back to you with another chance to chase it. They will learn this as time goes on. Throwing the ball again will be the reward for bringing the ball promptly back to you. In the meantime, do all you can to make it rewarding for the puppy to bring the ball to you. Pet, praise and play gentle tug-of-war games with the ball, letting him win (for now). Trade the ball for another ball, which you will roll. Or, you could trade the ball for a little dog treat. If the puppy shows absolutely no interest in the ball whatsoever, just ignore that. Do not talk to him, or say "get it." and do not play with or touch the pup. If he does not show any interest for several minutes, end the session, get up and walk away. Soon the pup will learn that ball time is fun time, attention time and play time, while non-ball time is dull and boring.

A rolling ball stimulates the prey drive in this puppy.

Some puppies show an interest in chasing the ball and picking it up but not in bringing it back. To remedy this, shorten the distance he can move away from you with the ball. Try moving to the end of the hall and sitting an arm's length away from the wall. When he picks up the ball, you will be right there to take it from his mouth and give him another one, or a treat. My youngest puppy, Koda, had this problem. In addition to not being all that interested in the ball, he wouldn't return it "to hand." I worked on rewarding the "give" command when he released it into my hand. This is outlined in Chapter 4, "Flyball Basics." I shaped the behavior of releasing the ball to me by rewarding him each time he dropped it in my hand. The trick is to get your hand on the ball (in the pup's mouth) and have a treat ready to give instantly. The puppy usually lets go of the ball upon seeing the treat. Only reward the "give" if your hand is on the ball when the pup releases it. Timing is important if you are going to use shaping. The end result is that the puppy learns that a ball in the hand (your hand) is worth a nice treat. After this, he will try to present you with the ball to get the treat.

A good exercise to practice this involves getting five balls and placing them on the floor around you. I use the words, "Get your ball!" You could use, "Pick it up," or anything you plan to say when your dog is older and you want him to pick up and give you the ball. I also use a hand signal. I shrug my shoulders and show both of my empty palms with my fingers spread. It's kind of an, "I don't know where it is," gesture. A puppy that is beginning to understand the "ball is worth one treat" equation will soon be picking up a ball to exchange it for a goodie. If the pup offers other types of learned behaviors in an effort to get the treat, like speaking, waving or rolling over, don't be suckered by his cute antics. You must reward only the correct answer to the question, "Where's your ball?" If you have to cheat and help him by pointing or grabbing a ball and rolling it a little, that's all right. After a few rewards for correct behavior, any bright pup will be collecting those balls and giving them to you faster than you can grab the treats. The lesson we have taught here is: It's okay to give up the ball.

Box Play

It is not too early to start work with the box, even if your puppy is still getting used to retrieving the ball. Depending on the type of Flyball box you have, you can place the puppy's food dish on top of it. You can set treats on top of it. Any time your pup voluntarily goes near the box to investigate, praise the dog.

Practice triggering the box some distance away to get the puppy used to the sound. Try pairing the sound with something pleasant, like eating, whenever possible. If the puppy already likes the ball, you can load one into the cup and trigger the box yourself so that your dog can see the ball coming out at him. Border Collie puppies like this game so much they come back with the ball and sometimes act as if they would try to reload it themselves! This is because they are highly intelligent and very curious about the funny hole in the box that unexpectedly throws out tennis balls. Soon, as the pup starts approaching boldly and climbs on the box, you can begin rewarding pedal contact by tossing the ball to him when his foot happens to touch the pedal. Even a light brush is rewarded initially—remember we are "shaping" here. When the puppy starts realizing that something he is doing at the box is causing a ball to be tossed or rolled down the front of the box, he will intentionally start trying to make contact with the pedal.

The owner has rolled a ball up the face of the Flyball box. In chasing it, the puppy has landed on the pedal. This is to get the puppy used to making contact with the box.

In a tournament, the fast dogs hit the box hard, flip themselves inside out and race back in the other direction. One thing you can do with the puppies that carries over into adulthood is to teach them to hit the box with turning around in mind. They need to learn to shove off *as* they trigger the pedal. To do this, take your pup up to the box and show the ball in your hand. Let him watch you toss the ball toward the face of the box. This works best with the triangle-shaped boxes, where the whole front is a 45-to 70-degree-angle pedal. The puppy will jump at the ball, but by the time he lands on the box pedal, the ball will have bounced backwards and the dog must push backwards to catch it. This all-in-one "pounce and turn" maneuver will lead to super-quick turns later on when the puppy learns to trigger the box without human help.

The young puppy's bones have not developed well enough to put together the pieces of Flyball racing, but pups can learn many of the individual steps in preparation for adulthood. Here are some of the parts to Flyball training, broken down to what you can do with and expect from a young puppy.

Prepping

Get your pup used to the words used in Flyball racing. Whenever you throw a ball, get the dog psyched by saying, "Ready? Ready?" When you practice your restrained Recalls and Send Aways, use, "On your mark, get set . . . GO!"

The owner letting the puppy go for a restrained Send Away to a friend who is bouncing a ball. *Joanne Weber*

Release

Get the dog focused on the end of the runway, whether it is on a friend, the Flyball box or a ball (no jumps). Your pup will run straight away when released. Make sure all eyes are on the target. If the dog is looking off to the side, aim the pup's face at the target with your hands. Don't be too far away from the target at first. Start with short distances so he will not take two steps and turn around to see where you are.

Passing

With the puppies on leash, practice making an elongated, counter-clockwise loop on a 4-foot-wide section of mat. Puppies walk in the center of the mat; handlers walk on the outside at the edge of the mat. Start at a walk, build up to a trot, and then a run, with the puppies passing each other going and coming. They need to get used to seeing other dogs running around.

The owner is playing "chase me" (restrained Recall) with "Tango," a Jack Russell Terrier puppy. *Joanne Weber*

Speed

The puppy may still be too tiny to be very coordinated or agile, but you can practice restrained Recalls and "chase me" games. Have someone hold your puppy as you run down the mat calling the dog. You can throw or roll a ball at the end when your dog catches up with you.

Box Approach, Hitting Pedal, Coming Off Box

Most of the tips for starting the puppy on the box in the previous section apply here. Practice tossing the ball so that it bounces off the box, as described earlier.

Catching

Many young puppies lack the mouth/eye coordination needed to catch a ball in the air. Some puppies do not realize at first that they can catch a ball in the air. To teach them that they can catch a ball from the air, begin by holding the ball above their noses so that they have to lunge to grasp it. After taking it from your hand in this manner, you can begin dropping the ball into the pup's mouth, just before her teeth are clamped down on it. Pups feel more confident about catching it in mid-air after doing this.

Next, you need to make the pup want to catch it in mid-air. Lob the ball up so it bounces several times, tossing it only a very short distance. The puppy will have several good opportunities to nab the ball as it arcs up and comes down. You may see your puppy seem to "bounce" with the ball at first until she gets coordinated enough to really catch. Another way to create interest in catching is to double-bounce the ball from the floor to a wall, or lob the ball off a wall. The more times the ball bounces, the more interesting it is, the slower it travels and the more chances the dog has to catch it in the air. After your puppy gets interested enough to want to catch the ball, and is trying to catch it, toss a ball directly to the dog. Sit or stand a short distance directly in front of him and lob it right to the puppy. Make a big fuss if he manages to catch it.

Grounders

The puppy will get practice getting grounders when you introduce the rolling ball and practice the "Where's your ball?" game.

Jumping

I do not recommend introducing the rigors of jumping until your puppy's bones have matured. However, the pup would normally run and play in the course of growing up, and to encourage "structured" running will not pose any detriment to the puppy. I have cut slots out of a 5-inch-high piece of 2 by 6, which will hold a 1-, 2- or 4-inch board. When you toss a ball down the mat, the puppy will just run over these boards like they were nothing. The puppy is not actually jumping, but learning to run or walk over obstacles in the way rather than walking around them. This helps build the puppy's timing and stride length.

"Murphy," owned by Claudia Burgdorf, is learning to go over obstacles in his path with single strides by using these low puppy jumps as cavaletti.

Singles

As the puppy comes to accept these white strips, begin spacing them out so that one stride equals one jump.

How far apart the boards are placed depends on your puppy's size and stride length. For example, a three-month-old Border Collie puppy may use the 1-inch or 2-inch boards, spaced 5 feet apart. A four-month-old may be ready to start hopping over 4-inch boards, spaced 6 feet apart. The height is not as important as the spacing between the jumps right now. The board only has to be high enough to make the puppy step over them, rather than landing on them or running into them. The distance between the jumps should be set so that there is only one stride between each. The jumps aren't really to be jumped at this point, they are just to help dogs get their stride—like using cavaletti. As the puppy grows bigger and the stride distance increases, move the jumps farther and farther apart.

Finish Line and Follow Through

Using bare mats, or the tiny puppy cavaletti, your restrained Recalls should involve getting the dog to run past the finish line. Throw or roll a ball for him to chase, so he keeps going. Don't teach him to come to a screeching halt when he gets just past the finish line or when he gets to you.

The puppy runs back over the baby jumps for a ball.

Exposure

Bring the puppy to practice so that he can get used to the noise and chaos of dogs running all over and barking excitedly.

Whether you follow these training guidelines or not, get your puppy out to Flyball practice. Have your dog get used to playing with other dogs before and after practice. Expose the dog to the noise and confusion of competition. Many people underestimate the ability of young puppies to learn, or feel that training should not commence until the dog is more physically and mentally mature. My feelings are that as long as you are making this a game, and not creating any pressure to perform, the puppy will not be stressed by the training. Introduction to "real" jumping at the lowest height should not begin until the dog is at least six months old, and much older with some breeds. A dog must be at least one year old to begin Flyball competition, so there's no need to rush the real jumps any sooner than those little bones can handle it.

By showing the young puppy the rudimentary components of Flyball, you will have less work for yourself and fewer corrections to make when the dog gets older and is ready for advanced training.

It is important to warm up your dog before beginning any strenuous physical activity like Flyball racing. Some stretching and a game of fetch will get the dog's muscles moving. Karli is "consumer testing" a new dog toy for Karla Kimmey. The new product was "Border Collie approved," of course! This item can be ordered through Legacy by Mail, 296-C Alamaha St., Kahului, HI 96732. *Terry Ryan*

Chapter 12

Conditioning Your Dog for Flyball Racing

As with any physically demanding sport, you will want to make sure that your dog is in good physical condition before you expose it to the rigors of training. Dogs perform best when they are in fit condition. You may have to put your dog on a special diet and program of regular exercise before you start training, but it will be worth the wait. If it is a chore for him to just run down and back over the jumps, Flyball training will seem more like work than play. If your pup is in optimum physical condition, there will be less chance of injury, and the dog will learn to enjoy this new activity.

Regular team practice is important. If your team is able to practice one or two times a week, your dog will be prepared for the energy requirements for an actual competition. When practicing each week, remember to try to emulate what would actually transpire at a tournament. For example, if competitions in your area commonly use the best three out of five racing format, you will want to practice running two warm-up runs and at least five heats of actual racing. This way, you will get an idea of your dog's endurance. If your Corgi "poops out" after three races, you can either try to build endurance or plan to have a backup small dog to give the other a chance to rest.

My team does not practice right before a tournament. Since our practice night is Friday, I feel that the dogs should have a break and not run the night before a tournament. If the practice night was earlier in the week, it wouldn't make that much difference. In fact, depending on whether or not the team really needs the practice, I sometimes opt for a

Wednesday practice during the week before a tournament. People have varying theories on the amount of rest a dog should have prior to competition. You should use what works best for you and your team.

In between practices, you should not let your dogs become inactive. If you practice for Flyball only once a week, you should exercise your dog with a ball, flying disk or water retrieving dummy on "off" days. Going for a walk on a leash is not the same as running, jumping or playing in the water. The latter forms of exercise more closely compare to the kind of physical workout your dog would get at Flyball practice.

Just as with any physical workout for humans, dogs need a stretching and warm-up period to prepare muscles for actual exercise. In addition, after a physical workout, your dog should be given another opportunity for stretching and cooling down to prevent blood from pooling in the extremities and excess lactic acid building up in the tissues, which can cause cramping and muscle soreness.

When Flyball teams arrive at tournaments, they group their people together in their crating area and watch the schedule to see when they will race next. Many times, people overlook the importance of taking dogs out of the crate and giving them a chance to work their muscles prior to racing. It is a good idea to take a ball or a toy outside and let your dog have a good warm-up session before racing. It is important for these dogs to have a chance to stretch their muscles and move their joints before the official warm up over the jumps.

Routine Maintenance

In addition to keeping your dog's muscles, heart and lungs conditioned with regular exercise, it is important to perform regular grooming and maintenance.

All dogs' toenails should be kept short and checked every week or two. If a dog's nail splits, it is extremely painful. Nail trimming should be done far enough in advance of the tournament so that the dog is used to the feel of shorter nails and so that in case you accidentally cut the quick when trimming a nail, it will have time to heal and not break open again while racing.

To help your dog get better traction, the hair between the pads of the feet should be trimmed. Once again, it is better if this is done in advance of the tournament to avoid the chance of nicking the dog with scissors or having the dog feel short, bristly hairs between the toes. Some handlers also use preparations to make the paws more "tacky" and less likely to slide on the mats or the box surface. And, with some dogs, it is necessary to wrap the carpal area with a stretch athletic bandage like Vet Wrap® to prevent the dogs from tearing or abrading their dewclaws when they slide to a stop at the box. This should be done right before the tournament and must be inspected by the judge before the dog races. The reason for this is to ensure that the wrap is a preventative measure, and not a bandage to cover an injury sustained during the tournament. Dogs are not allowed to race if they are otherwise bandaged or injured.

This Golden Retriever wears athletic stretch bandage on his legs to protect the small pads on the back of his pasterns. *Joanne Weber*

When grooming the dog before a tournament, check for overall good health. Your dog won't feel much like racing with a sore mouth, an ear infection, impacted anal sacs or an upset stomach. In addition, be sure to check for mats or foreign objects in the hair. Mats in a sensitive area, like the "armpit," pull the hair each time the dog stretches out, causing discomfort.

Be careful when exercising your dog at Flyball tournaments. Often, the only place to take your dog is a paved parking lot. Do not let your dog run on asphalt as it will scrape the pads right off the feet. The pad leather peels right back, creating a painful condition. If this ever happens, you have to wait for new pads to grow. The old pads will just slough off. If this occurs, keep your dog from running as much as possible and protect those tender feet. A dog with these pad problems will not be running for Flyball until he heals.

Chapter 13

High-tech
Flyball

F lyball has evolved steadily over the past ten years. Although the basics of the sport have remained the same, there are new training techniques, new equipment and new technology for going "beyond the basics." Flyball has become a high-tech sport.

In the old days, people threw a box together in the garage, taught their dog to operate it, added some jumps and, voila, they had a Flyball dog. If that dog could run down over the jumps, hit the box, catch the ball and run back to finish in seven seconds or so, it was even better. If they did this with three more dogs, they had a Flyball team. If this team entered a competition, they might have been really "hot" and only lost a few seconds on passes. They might have won the tournament with times clocked on the stopwatch in the 29 or 30 second range.

Mechanical Technology

Well, gone are the days of the box thrown together in the garage. The Flyball boxes used today in competition are, for the most part, made commercially. The older, catapult-style boxes made with pulleys, string, latches and bungie cords are history. The new boxes have more straightforward releasing systems, steeper angles, larger pedals and enclosed cups. They are built by people who have found a way to package reliability, speed, precision, durability, ease of operation and aesthetics into one product that sells for $150 to $350. Of course, you will buy not one, but at least two of these boxes because you need a backup in case of a malfunction or if you have two teams that would end up running against each other.

Training Technology

Passed also are the days of the formula that:

dog does box + dog does jumps = dog does Flyball.

I'm not sure what kind of formulas other teams use, but I have broken down the Flyball race into over 25 separate parts that must be taught to the dog and worked on before that dog is deemed ready to race. These are described in detail in Chapter 15, "Performance Checklist." The separate parts of Flyball are introduced to the dogs one at a time. The parts of training are done in reverse order (backward behavior chaining) so that everything gets easier for the dog as the training progresses toward the start. Even when the training is complete, the finished product is put together only to get team times, practice team passing or otherwise prepare for a tournament.

The Head Judge, Kevin Hughs, gets ready to initiate the timing sequence on the Electronic Judging System.

Electronic Technology

In today's competitions, you will seldom see a dog run seven seconds. You will also rarely see teams waste two seconds on their passes. And the days when you would hope to beat the stopwatch to bring in times under 32

The Electronic Judging System lights. The top center light is the blue standby (system on) light. Each side then has (from top to bottom) a red passing light, two yellow lights (ready . . . set . . .), the green (go!) light and a red (false start indicator) light.

seconds (so you could get the Flyball title point) are long gone. For that matter, so are the stopwatches.

For the past several years, Flyball enthusiasts in North America have been able to use state-of-the-art technology: an electronic starting light system (like they use in drag racing). That's right. They've even replaced the old, "On your mark, get set . . . GO!" Now the head judge just makes sure the teams are ready and then indicates that the Electronic Judging System countdown has been initiated. He or she will do this with a gesture and/or a comment like, "We're racing," or a blast from the whistle. Then it is up to the first dog and handler to watch the lights.

The Electronic Judging System does most of the work for the line judges. The system starts when the blue light comes on as the warning light, then yellow, yellow . . . GREEN! And they're off! If one or the other (or both) of the dogs in first position false starts, an electric eye (laser beam) senses it and a red light at the bottom comes on, stopping the race and indicating which lane false started. It is not the judge's responsibility to watch the dogs, but rather to watch the lights for a false start. The head judge will blow the whistle twice to indicate a false start, and will restart the race. In the event of a premature pass, the red passing light at the top will come on. Then, the line judge raises a flag, just like the old days before timing lights. In addition, the passing lights (a second row of laser beams) can detect premature passes among the next three dogs.

Line judges don't have to do much but keep their eyes on the lights and push a button to finish the race. The "finish" button they push tells the EJS to stop the clock when the next dog's nose crosses a beam, and both teams' times are displayed to be recorded at the head table. The line judge is no longer responsible for stopping the time the instant the dog's nose crosses the finish.

What kinds of times are recorded? The three top teams that take turns setting and breaking new world records are running in the 17 second range. The more sophisticated training methods, the better Flyball boxes, the EJS and the dedicated, competitive attitudes of the people in the sport have made the teams faster and faster. I can remember when everyone thought that it was impossible for a team to finish in less than 20 seconds. We all thought that was as good as it could get. That's four dogs each running under 5 seconds, with perfect passes. Now, we have dozens of teams, representing the top Flyball clubs in North America, running under 20 seconds. The fastest time on record as of this writing is 16.96, run by Instant Replay, a Canadian team.

Computer Technology

The numbers of Flyball enthusiasts have increased dramatically. At this writing, there are over 430 teams, representing roughly 100 Flyball clubs in competition. Twelve years ago, there were only about 10 teams in competition. With the increase in numbers, the organizational paperwork has become mind-boggling.

The North American Flyball Association has its own computer programs to keep records organized. The NAFA computer is fed the tournament results and tabulates the title points earned by each individual dog. It then automatically prints a certificate if a dog has achieved any title with the number of points accumulated.

NAFA must keep track of each team's participation in sanctioned tournaments, including the team's average time and fastest time recorded. Each team is seeded (ranked) according to their best time. Each team is periodically sent a breakdown of the team's history, showing each individual dog's record, accumulated Flyball points, titles earned and certificates issued. Also, a computer printout is made available that shows the various breeds involved in the sport everywhere, the total number of dogs of each breed, and how many of them have achieved titles of FD, FDX and FDCh. At the end of the year, the number of times each team entered and hosted tournaments is calculated to determine the number of delegate votes allotted to each club for the coming year. Without computer technology it would be difficult to run an organization of this size.

And, of course, now we have Flyball on the Internet. If you would like to exchange ideas, funny stories, brags, congratulations or anything else with fellow Flyball enthusiasts, you need only to get yourself online and join the Flyball bulletin board. You can subscribe to the Flyball mailing list by sending an e-mail to listproc@ces.com. Include your e-mail address and the words "subscribe Flyball" in your message. You can also access the World Wide Web site for information on the sport of Flyball at: http://www.cs.umn.edu/~ianhogg/Flyball/Flyball.html. By accessing the home page, you can get all kinds of information related to Flyball, like upcoming tournament dates, a NAFA directory and the NAFA newsletter.

Chapter 14

Rules of Competition with NAFA

The purpose of this book is to help people learn about the sport of Flyball. The North American Flyball Association (NAFA) has its own Rules and Policies booklet, which is a very comprehensive manual, covering every aspect of the rules. A copy can be obtained by sending $15 in American funds to NAFA Inc., 1400 W. Devon Ave., Box 512, Chicago, IL 60660. For simplicity, I have included only the rules for competition. These are reprinted with permission from Chapter 6 of the NAFA Rules and Policies booklet.

Rules for Competition

Section 6.1—Amateur Competition

The NAFA encourages amateur competition. Teams may accept up to $500.00 per event per day and/or trophies, uniforms and equipment that identify a sponsor or host club. Individuals or teams that accept money or other compensation for Flyball™ competition or demonstrations over the amount specified above may not compete in NAFA sanctioned competition.

Section 6.2—Teams

(a) The NAFA Regular class of competition includes teams made up of any type or breed of dog including those of mixed or unknown parentage and **must be offered at every tournament.**

(b) A non-regular class (multibreed, pee-wee, veterans, etc.) is any class other than the NAFA Regular class.

(c)   In multibreed competition, teams can consist of different breeds recognized by any Kennel Club or Stud Book, or one dog of mixed breed parents. Any deviation from this policy must be stated on the tournament's promotional flyer and have approval from the Regional Director.

(d)   Dogs may not compete in more than one class at a NAFA sanctioned tournament except;

  (i)   When a tournament is unlimited.

  (ii)   When a limited entry tournament does not fill.

(e)   If a dog has raced in a NAFA sanctioned tournament, the dog may not race with another team for **four** (4) months. Any deviation from this rule requires the team to run "non-competitive" and no NAFA points will be awarded. Exceptions are as follows and must be approved by the Regulatory Committe:

  (i)   The handler/dog has moved to another area.

  (ii)   A team agrees to dissolve.

  (iii)   A new team is formed. Once a dog has joined a team, that dog may not run with another team, new or existing, for a period of **four** (4) months. A team is considered to be "new" until they race in their first NAFA™ sanctioned tournament.

Section 6.16—Rules of Racing

(a)   The Start: Dogs may start from a stationary or running start. When using a manual start (Head Judge's whistle), any part of the dog's body, whether in the air or on the ground, or if the handler's feet are over the line before the whistle is blown, will be an infraction, to be called by the Line Judge or Head Judge. When electronic starting lights are used, any part of the dog's or handler's body breaking the beam will cause an infraction to be called by the Line Judge or Head udge. The heat is to be restarted. If a second such infraction is called against the same team (for that heat) the dog must be run again. If a second false start is called coincidental with the opposing teams first false start, the heat is to be restarted.

(b)   The Run: Each dog is to hurdle the four jumps in succession, trigger the box and return over all four jumps with the ball. Only when any part of the first dog's body has reached the start/finish line, (on the ground or in the air), may any part of the second dog's body reach the start/finish line. Generally this is a nose to nose pass at the start/finish line This is the same for all four dogs as well as dogs that must run again. Early passes will be indicated by the Line Judge and the dog will be required to run again after the other dogs have run. If a dog reaches the start/finish line before the preceding dog has reached the start/finish line, or does not take every jump, or does not trigger the box, or takes the ball from the cup, or does not return with the ball, the dog must run again. If the handler's foot crosses the start/finish line during his/her dog's run, the dog must run again (with the exception of setting up a knocked down jump or retrieving a loose ball).

(c) Knocked down jumps: A dog that knocks down a jump during a run shall not be penalized, provided the dog(s) clear the jump as if it were standing. A "runner" or handler may set up knocked down jumps if doing so does not interfere with or guide the dog in any way.

(d) Box Malfunction: The box loader shall indicate to the box judge when there is a box malfunction. The heat shall be stopped. The Head Judge is to examine the box. If, in the opinion of the Head Judge, the box has malfunctioned, the heat shall be run again. If the box is found to be working, then the heat shall be forfeited. If another box is not available and the box cannot be repaired in a reasonable time, the heat and any remaining heats are to be forfeited. If the box malfunctions a second time (or the spare box malfunctions) in the same race, the heat shall be forfeited and all remaining heats in that race shall be forfeited.

(e) Intervention: Should the ball bounce back into the cup as the dog tries to catch it, the box loader may reset the box for the dog to trigger it (without penalty). This is the only time at which the box loader is permitted to signal a dog to push the pedal.

(f) Fouling: If a dog relieves itself in the ring, the team forfeits the heat.

(g) Out-of-Bounds/ Out-Of-Play: The host club shall specify the race area boundaries. If a ball bounces out of bounds and the dog retrieves the ball unaided, there shall be no penalty. If the dog is aided by a spectator, handler, box loader or other, the dog is to run again.

Out-of-play shall be the same as if the ball were out of bounds; for example, if the ball becomes lodged or trapped inside the box.

(h) Conduct of the Box Loader: Except during the warm-up, to retrieve a loose ball or get a fresh supply of balls to load, the box loader must remain in the upright position behind the box, and may offer verbal encouragement only, as long as such encouragement does not distract the opposing team. The box loader is to remain in position until the outcome of the heat is determined by the Head Judge. If, in the judge's opinion, a box loader has violated any of these rules, his/her team may forfeit the heat. If, in the opinion of the judge, a box loader assists a dog, except where provided for in the rules, the dog shall run again.

The Head Judge indicates the winner of the heat.

(i) Interference: If a dog or any team member interferes with the opposing team during a heat, the team causing the interference will forfeit the heat. This includes interference in the racing lane, in all in-bounds areas, and in the area where dogs are waiting to run. Interference is defined as obstructing the other team's dog from running its race. A dog chasing a loose ball into the other team's area is not necessarily interference.

(j) The finish: The first team to have all four dogs successfully complete a run wins the heat. The finish shall be when the last of the four dogs reaches the finish line with any part of its body, in the air or on the ground. A tournament may be won due to default by the opposing team according to the rules of racing.

(k) Distractions: Team members shall not distract the opposing team by bouncing balls, using a Flyballbox at the end of the run, or by any other means nor throw any object for their dogs (i.e. balls, toys, Frisbees, dummies, gloves or treats). Team members are required to pick up any loose balls. The first offense of these infractions shall receive a warning—a second offense or any offense thereafter during the race will result in the loss of the heat.

(l) Broken boards: The heat shall not be stopped for broken boards unless, in the opinion of the Head Judge, the dog(s) may be subject to injury. If the heat is stopped by the Head Judge to prevent a possible injury, the heat is to be restarted.

Section 6.17—Aggressive dogs

If a dog shows undue aggression toward another dog or handler at any time during the competition, the Head Judge may excuse the dog from competing and a standby dog is to be used. The degree of aggression that warrants substitution is to be determined by the Head Judge. Any dog excused from competition must be reported to the NAFA. At the second such report, the dog will be barred from future competition. An application for reinstatement may be submitted after a period of one year.

Section 6.18—Lame Dogs, Bitches in Season, Dogs Recovering from Surgery, Leg Wrapping

Wrap on dog's legs may be used with the prior approval of the Head Judge.

If, in the opinion of the Head Judge, a dog is lame, in season, recovering from surgery or for a related reason should not compete, the same shall be excused from competition.

Section 6.19—Record Times

Video recorded record-breaking times shall be reviewed by the Board of Directors. The video recorder shall be set on the line. Only video recorded record-breaking times can be verified by the Board of Directors. Record-breaking times not recorded on video in the described manner will not be recognized by the NAFA as a NAFA record.

The North American Flyball Association

The North American Flyball Association was organized to oversee the sport of Flyball. Its aim is to promote cooperation and good sportsmanship and to further the sport of Flyball racing. Over the years, NAFA has worked hard to further define the rules of racing and to develop a comprehensive rule book which includes guidelines for every aspect of sanctioned competition.

NAFA is run by a Board of Directors, consisting of nine Officers. The Board meets regularly to discuss rules and policies amendments, guidelines, and other activities. The meetings are usually held in conjunction with a tournament where many of the Board members would already be in attendance.

Board members serve a three year term, and are elected by the delegates (members of active Flyball teams). Anyone who would like to run for election to the Board of Directors should submit their name to the nominating committee, along with biographical information.

Becoming a NAFA Judge

Interested persons are encouraged to become NAFA Judges. To become an approved NAFA Judge, you must be at least 18 years of age. Applicants must have experience by apprenticing at a sanctioned tournament or attending a judging seminar. After judging several tournaments as a probationary judge, the applicant will be voted on by the Board of Directors for approval as a Head Judge.

The following "Judges Guidelines" are reprinted, with permission, from the NAFA Rules and Policies guidebook:

Section 6.6—Judges Guidelines

(a) Judges should be friendly and courteous, even sympathetic, but above all impartial and firm. Judges must have a thorough understanding gained through personal experience. A judge must be familiar with the regulations, rules and requirements.

(b) The judge's responsibility also extends to the exhibitors, to the host club or organization, to the spectators and sponsors. A judge must be arbiter and diplomat. A judge must leave exhibitors and spectators with the feeling that each team was given an equal opportunity and no team was given an unfair advantage.

(c) A judge is not to engage in conversation with a disgruntled exhibitor.

(d) Upon arriving at the site, a judge shall immediately report to the tournament director. A judge should be at his/her ring at least 30 minutes before the competition, to check the ring, jumps, matting and backdrops. If dogs are to be measured and boxes inspected before the competition, the judge should allow additional time as directed by the tournament director.

(e) The Rules and Policies are a basic guide. They should not be considered a manual containing explicit direction for every possible situation. Judgment calls should be based on the experience, good character, and fairness of the judge. The intelligent application of discretionary authority demands that a judge exercise common sense, fairness and initiative. **Above all else, the safety and well-being of the dogs and exhibitors shall be foremost.**

The Head Judge, Dave Samuels, indicates a no finish for the team in the far lane.

(f) Prior to the scheduled time for competition, the Head Judge must inspect the ring. It should meet all of the requirements of the regulations. The start/finish line shall be clearly marked. Jump placement, jump heights, backstops, barriers, and box location should be measured to make sure they meet the requirements of the regulations. A deviation of one-quarter inch on the jump heights is considered minor, and acceptable. Each box shall be inspected by the panel of judges and shall not be allowed if, in the opinion of the panel of judges, the box has been constructed or altered in a manner that does not meet the box requirements.

(g) The Head Judge shall measure dogs jumping less than 16 inches, if time allows. Otherwise, it will be up to the discretion of the team whether to have their dogs measured or not prior to the competition. If the judge is uncertain of the dog's height after three accurate measurements, the height measurement shall be moved to the lower height, for the benefit of the dog. However, if the Head Judge later determines that the team is not jumping the proper height (in a round-robin tournament), the team will forfeit any races won at the incorrect jump height or the team will be excused (in a single or double elimination tournament). The Head Judge may at any time measure a dog. However, once a dog is measured by the Head Judge, the Head Judge is under no obligation to measure the same dog again. If, after a dog is measured and the Head Judge determines he has made a mistake, the team shall in no way be penalized, however the team will be required to jump the proper height for any remaining heats. Any protest with respect to a dog's jump height must be verbalized within 30 minutes of the heat in question.

(h) The Head Judge shall stop the heat for interference, fouling in the ring or undue aggression by dog or competitor, and award that heat to the competing team.

(i) Line Judges shall:

1. Record which dogs participate in every heat using NAFA Time Sheet, form C-2.

2. Stop the race for the first false start, for which the heat is to be restarted.

3. Indicate with a signal when a dog is to run again (early pass, missed jump, crossing the finish line without the ball, or if the handler crosses the start/finish line during the heat (other than to set up a knocked down jump or to retrieve a loose ball), or other rule violations for which a dog must run again.

(j) Determining the winner of a heat.

1. When a heat is judged using the Electronic Judging System, the winner of close heats shall be determined based on the Electronic Judging System times. When the times are within .003 of a second (for example, a time of 21.798 versus 21.801), the Head Judge shall declare the race to be a tie.

2. When a heat is judged to be a tie using manual judging (in the absence or failure of the Electronic Judging System), the judge's decision shall be unanimous with respect to determining winners of close heats and shall be based on their visual view of the finish line, not on the clocks. If the judges are not in agreement, the Head Judge shall consult with the Line Judges and either declare a winner, or declare the heat to be a tie or a dead heat.

(k) Judges shall not assist teams during warm-ups.

These two dogs know their jobs and are both focused on what they are supposed to do rather than worrying about each other.

Chapter 15

Performance
Checklist

To have a team perform at optimum levels of precision, all of the dogs should be doing each of the separate parts extremely well. If the dog is introduced to Flyball by the methods in this book, you should be able to avoid many of the problems that will produce a less-than-perfect performance. On my Flyball team, all participants are required to train in the prescribed manner to achieve the desired results. There will always be those people, however, who want to skip steps or who think their dogs are doing better than they actually are. There will be people who think their dog is trained and doesn't need to come to practice regularly because he "knows it."

No matter how well people think their dog knows the parts of Flyball, it is always important to practice with the team. And sometimes the person who owns the dog is not the best judge of how well the dog is doing. Some people think their own dog is a shining star and won't benefit from regular practice.

Every dog and handler can improve somewhere. If your dog's performance is flawed in any area, you become a handicap to the team. Once a dog learns the basics of Flyball racing, he is not ready for competition until all of the items on this checklist can be performed with no problem. Your dog might be really fast, but may have this slight problem passing, so he can only run last. Wrong answer. The dog needs to get over the passing problem before he can be of use to the team.

Does your dog really understand all of the parts of the game? If this were school, would she be getting an A+ on all of the following parts? If so, then your dog is ready for competition with the team. He will be an asset to your team, and not a liability.

Evaluating Performance

The following parts of Flyball racing and descriptions of optimum performance expected in each area are for use in evaluation. A dog not meeting the standard of performance should receive additional training. Consult the chapter on the training steps, or the chapter on problem solving to get the dog performing to the desired level.

Preparation to Start

When you say the cue words, "Ready?" and "Get Your Ball" (or whatever you use), the dog gets really excited. He is focused on the Flyball box and poised to take off at a dead run. He is straining to go and can hardly be contained.

Release

When you let the dog go, she remains focused on the box and bursts to maximum speed as fast as possible.

Start

The dog does not hesitate as he approaches the starting line. The dog reaches the line as the light turns green (or on "go") if he is the first dog or for a perfect "no daylight" pass with the another dog.

Pass (Handler Timing)

The handler's release is timed perfectly with the returning dog's position to enable the two dogs to cross nose-to-nose at the start. The handler knows where she is releasing the dog and can do it in the same manner each time.

Pass (Dog Focus)

The dog remains focused on the box and does not try to slow down because he is concerned about running into the other dog. He does not look at, or try to go after, the dog returning.

Speed (Going)

The dog races down all four jumps at maximum speed, stretching out and using a minimum of effort to clear the jumps.

Approaching Box
The dog should not slow down or stop to touch the pedal of the box.

Hitting Pedal
The dog should "bounce" off the pedal, using it to stop his forward momentum and turn himself for the return over the jumps.

Catching
The dog should snatch the ball while bouncing off the pedal and turning. He should not stop to mouth or chew the ball.

"Koda," the author's Border Collie, ricochets off the pedal as he catches the ball.

Coming Off the Box
The dog should fling himself off the box, ideally in the same direction each time, and should do so with a 180-degree turn. He should not make a wide U-turn, but rather should turn (like a swimmer's turn) and use his back legs to kick off from the box and get the drive necessary to be propelled toward the no. 4 jump.

Fielding Grounders
If the dog fumbles the ball, he should scoop it up quickly and continue racing toward the finish.

Angle Jumping the No. 4 Jump

If the ball rolls out of the racing lane, the dog should be able to retrieve it and still make sure he heads straight back for the no. 4 jump.

Jumping

The dog should not miss or knock down any jumps. He should not break boards or "bounce" over the jumps, but rather should clear them with a minimum of effort. If you watch a really good Flyball dog race down the course, you will barely see his back move up and down. It will look almost like the dog's body remains level, but he is picking up his legs to clear the jumps.

It is best if the dog takes off and lands about the same distance from either side of the jump as opposed to leaping too early and landing just inches on the other side of each jump, which expends too much energy and is dangerous.

Speed (Returning)

The dog should run equally fast going and coming. He should be firmly focused on the target and concentrate on getting back to it as fast as possible.

This dog completely mastered the basics of Flyball during a five-day Dog Scout Camp. "Jacques," owned by Beth Duman, is doing single strides over all four jumps. Photo courtesy of Dog Scouts of America. *Joanne Weber*

Singles

The dog should be able to stretch out and do one pounce (a single stride) between each jump. Dogs under 13 inches at the shoulder may not be able to do singles.

Jump No. 1

The dog should not hesitate, slow down or run around the no. 1 jump.

Finish Line

The dog should keep up speed until he is far beyond the finish line, remaining focused on the target.

Passing (Traffic)

The returning dog should always come off slightly to his right (the owner's left) at the finish, and not barrel down the center of the mat where the next dog will be coming through. The owner of the returning dog needs to be off the mat so that the subsequent dog's owner can clearly judge the point at which he will release his dog.

Passing (Focus)

The returning dog should be focused on the target and not glancing over at the other team or the dog who is passing him.

Follow Through

After crossing the finish line, the dog should continue into the run-back area. Only there should he slow down.

Holding Ball

The dog should hold the ball into the run-back area and not spit it out until it is presented to the handler, or until the dog is invited by the handler to attack the target object.

Presenting Ball

If the dog uses food instead of a target, the ball should be held until it is traded to the owner for a treat.

Non-Aggression

No Flyball dog should pose a danger to any other handler or dog. Your dog must not be allowed to enter the other lane's run-back area or try to chase other dogs.

"Weasel" is getting ready to trade the ball for a treat, which is her real motivation for playing this game (besides being allowed to run and jump and bark). *Joanne Weber*

"Willie," a Jack Russell Terrier, attacks his target after a race. Like many Jack Russell owners, Rachel uses a ball on a rope to motivate Willie. He leaps for it, swings from it, and "kills" it—all very rewarding activities for a feisty terrier. *Joanne Weber*

Focus

A dog that isn't focused will not be good at any of these individual parts of Flyball training. Focus is the single most important part of the game. If your dog isn't driven to get something he cherishes at the finish line, then why should he pay attention? Focus is the first thing you need to get in Flyball training, and it will drive the dog through all of the parts of the behavior chain. Without it, your dog will never take the game seriously.

Non-Distractibility

Your dog should not be bothered by screaming fans, loose balls, interference from the other team or by seeing a family member in the audience. Focus should prevent him from noticing or caring about any of those things.

Dogs must be focused on the box and their target enough to ignore extraneous distractions.

Lane-Sureness

The dog should understand which lane he is racing in and never cross over to the other side, even if the ball goes way over by the other team's box.

Willingness to Run (For Anyone)

If your dog understands and loves the game, he should run Flyball for anyone. This will enable you to have more than one dog on a team, or have your dog attend a tournament when you can't go. It also comes in handy if you have a dog on two different teams that have to run against each other in a tournament.

The Border Collies in this picture are all owned by the author and run on the same team. Karli, Wile E. and Koda are being handled by fellow team members. They will run for anyone. Karli could start herself. She knows to go on "get set" when she is in first position, and she knows that her time to take off for a pass is when the returning dog is making his middle pounce.

Glossary of Flyball Terms

Breakout time   When the tournament director has set the division heats by team times, a breakout time is assigned. This is one second more than the best time submitted by the fastest seeded team in that division. If any team in the division runs faster than this time, they have broken out and they lose that heat. This rule was instituted to prevent sandbagging (see below).

Bye   In a double- or single-elimination competition, the top seeded teams sometimes get a bye, just as in other sports. This means they will not race the initial rounds of the elimination, but may run against the winner of race number one or two.

Captains' meeting   A meeting held before the start of a tournament, in which important information regarding the tournament is announced and racing sheets are handed out.

Clean run   A run in which a dog completes the course and brings back the ball without committing any rule infractions.

Dead heat   A heat that is so close that the two line judges and a referee cannot come to a unanimous decision as to who was the winner; therefore, it is a tie. When the EJS (see below) is used, the judge will look to the electronic readout to determine the winner. If the two times are within three one-hundredths of a second (like 19.986 and 20.012), the head judge will declare a tie.

Delegate   One or more members of a competing Flyball team, who get one vote per delegate to represent their team on any official NAFA voting or elections. The number of delegates each team gets is determined by the team's participation throughout the preceding year.

Division   A grouping of teams by their seed times for racing. They are ranked this way in an effort to make the racing closer, and more fair, when there is a wide diversity of team times.

Double elimination   A racing format where teams are seeded by times (or preliminary races) and race against other teams until they are defeated twice.

EJS   Electronic Judging System. Also called the passing lights, timing lights, or light system. The system consists of signal lights, laser beam sensors and a clock with digital readout. It starts and stops the race, records the times and detects false starts and early passes.

Exchange   The Canadian word for "pass," as in, "That was a perfectly timed exchange." (See *Pass*.)

Executive Director   The "Chief Executive Officer" of the North American Flyball Association.

False start   A situation when one or both teams' first dog crosses the starting line before the green light on the EJS starts the race. If it is the first false start for both teams, the race is then restarted.

FD   The Flyball Dog title, which is achieved by earning 20 title points in NAFA-sanctioned Flyball competitions.

FDX   The Flyball Dog Excellent title, which is achieved by earning 100 title points in NAFA-sanctioned Flyball competitions.

FDCh   The Flyball Champion title, achieved by earning 500 title points in NAFA-sanctioned Flyball competitions.

FM   The Flyball Master title, achieved by earning 5,000 title points in NAFA-sanctioned Flyball competitions.

FMX   The Flyball Master Excellent title, achieved by earning 10,000 title points in NAFA-sanctioned Flyball competitions.

FMCh   The Flyball Master Champion title, achieved by earning 15,000 title points in NAFA-sanctioned Flyball competitions.

FDGCh   The Flyball Grand Champion title, achieved by earning 30,000 title points in NAFA-sanctioned Flyball competitions.

Going "Hot" A term used to describe a dog that crossed the starting line prematurely, resulting in a red light, as in, "She went hot and we lost the race."

Hall of Fame The Flyball Hall of Fame is for dogs that have excelled consistently in Flyball competition. Nominations are screened by the NAFA Executive Committee and voted on by the delegates.

Heat One run between two teams. A race consists of three or more heats, depending on the racing format.

Interference The obstruction by one team of another team's run. This can be by another dog running across into the other team's racing lane, or by one team committing interference by distraction, such as not picking up their loose balls.

Invitational A competition in which the teams are asked to enter. NAFA does not sanction invitational events, as the rules state that all NAFA sanctioned events shall be open to ALL teams registered with NAFA.

Loser's bracket In a double-elimination tournament, this is where you go after you have lost a race. The winner of the loser's bracket will eventually come back to play the winner of the winner's bracket to determine the winner of the competition. This is like a consolation round in other sports.

Measure dog The smallest dog on your team, which allows the team's other dogs to jump a lower height.

No Finish (NF) A notation made on the official NAFA racing sheet to indicate that a team did not complete a heat.

No Time (NT) A notation made on the official NAFA racing sheet to indicate that no time was recorded because of a breakout, or a time did not get recorded and it was over 32 seconds. If a line judge gets a "no time" on a team due to a mistake on the judge's part (like not pushing the finish button on the EJS), then a time should be estimated and recorded so that team will not forfeit title points because of someone else's error.

Onyx Award A plaque given to honor dogs that have received 20,000 title points.

Out-of-play The area outside of the racing area boundaries. The head judge will declare whether or not a ball has gone out-of-play. If the ball goes out of bounds but the dog jumps the barrier, retrieves it and makes it back over all of the jumps without causing interference or getting assistance, it can still be considered "in play." A ball that falls down inside the Flyball box is considered out-of-play. If the ball accidentally bounces back into the cup, the loader is allowed to re-cock the box so the dog can trigger it again, and it is not considered a rule infraction.

Pass   When the outgoing and returning dog (ideally) meet at the start/finish line. Also called an "exchange."

Pass evaluator   The team member who stands at the start/finish line (somewhere behind the line judge) and lets the team members know how good or how bad their passes (or starts) were with some form of hand signals.

Qualifying round   The running of timed trials at a tournament to determine the seeding order for competition. This has pretty much been replaced by the honor system and the breakout rule.

Race   A set of heats run against another team.

Regional champion   The team that has consistently beaten other teams within its region for the year. To be a contender for Regional Champion, a club must compete in a minimum of four regional tournaments, each having at least 12 competing teams. There are fewer teams in existence for regions 6 and 9 only.

Regional director (RD)   A NAFA representative who is available to help teams within that region plan and hold Flyball tournaments. This individual is also there to help with the seeding and breaking of divisions. The RD also approves the tournament format.

Regions   Geographic divisions of North America for the purpose of regional competitions, assigning Regional Directors and determining Regional Champions.

Ring   The Flyball racing course. This includes the racing lanes, the area between them, the run-back area and everything else in bounds.

Round robin   A racing format in which each team will race against each other team in the division. The winning team would be the one that gained the most points for heats won.

Sandbagging   A term to describe the act of submitting estimated "best times" that are slower than what the team is actually running in order to make it easier to win. The breakout rule was devised to prevent sandbagging in that if a team runs faster than the time they have turned in, they will be penalized by automatically being declared the loser of the heat.

Seed   The ranking, by time, of the teams within a division for competition; the ranking of all of the teams competing in NAFA-sanctioned tournaments is available on a seed chart, which is put out in the newsletter every quarter.

Single elimination   A racing format whereby a team is eliminated after being beaten once. This format is usually used at the end of a tournament, after teams have raced for seeding positions for the finals.

Singles   A dog is said to be "doing singles" if it can take all four jumps with only one stride (pounce) between each jump.

Take-off point   The point at which you position your dog for a perfect pass or start to enable that dog to be at the start/finish line at the precise instant necessary and running at full speed. This point is usually somewhere between 15 and 20 feet from the start/finish line. This is the "where" that you can adjust if your pass is early or late.

Target   The motivation for your dog to play Flyball. Also referred to as the focus, or motivator. It is that thing the dog runs to earn.

Tie   A heat that is so close that a winner cannot be determined. A tied heat is usually rerun, depending on the tournament format and the system of assigning tournament points. The racing teams get to keep any title points earned for tied heats, as well as any heats which are run at the end of a tournament to break ties within divisions.

Timing point   The point when the returning dog is approximately 25 feet or less from finishing. This is the point that the next handler lets the dog go for a perfect pass at the start/finish line; also called the releasing point. This point has to be figured out for each two individual dogs, but is usually the middle pounce of the returning dog. This is the "when" you should never try to adjust if your pass is early or late.

Title points   The points that each individual dog on a team earns for each heat run, based on the team time (under 32.00 = 1 point; under

28.00 = 5 points; under 24.00 = 25 points). These points are accumulated and tabulated by NAFA for the awarding of titles to individual dogs.

Tournament director   The person who hosts a Flyball tournament, taking entries, delegating work and seeding teams, among other things.

Tournament points   The points that are won by a team in a competition, through round robin, double elimination or some other format. The tournament points determine the placements (winners) of each division in a tournament. There are different systems of assigning point values to wins, losses and ties, but it is usually one point for each race won.

Winner's bracket   In a double-elimination tournament, this is where a team stays as long as it continues to win. If a team ends up undefeated from the winner's bracket, it must race against the first-place team from the loser's bracket. If the undefeated team loses, the two teams must race again, as one team must be beaten twice (hence the term double elimination) before a winner can be determined.